THE ESSENTIAL RECIPES, TECHNIQUES
AND INGREDIENTS OF THAILAND

101 THAI DISHES
YOU NEED TO COOK
BEFORE YOU DIE

JET TILA

Celebrity Chef & Author

With **TAD WEYLAND FUKUMOTO**

Foreword by GUY FIERI

PAGE STREET
PUBLISHING CO.

PAGE STREET
PUBLISHING CO.

Distributed by Macmillan, sales in Canada by The Canadian Manda Group.

26   25   24   23   22   1   2   3   4   5

ISBN-13: 978-1-64567-366-8

ISBN-10: 1-64567-366-9

Library of Congress Control Number: 2021940668

Cover and book design by Meg Baskis for Page Street Publishing Co.

Photography by Ken Goodman

Printed and bound in the United States

THIS BOOK IS DEDICATED TO OUR PARENTS:

Mary and Pat Tila, and Myrtle and David Fukumoto.

CONTENTS

Foreword by Guy Fieri 7

Introduction 9

Pantry Breakdown 11

CURRIES & SOUPS: BOWLS OF YUM 19

My Favorite Northern Curry (Gaeng Hung Lay Moo) 21

Panang Curry Chicken (Gaeng Panang Gai) 22

Roast Duck Red Curry (Gaeng Phed Ped Yang) 25

Massaman Beef Curry (Gaeng Massamun Neau) 26

Curry Pastes from Scratch 28

    Red Curry Paste (Prik Gaeng Dang) 29

    Green Curry Paste (Prik Gaeng Keow) 29

    Yellow Curry Paste (Prik Gaeng Leung) 32

    Panang Curry Paste (Prik Gaeng Panang) 32

    Massaman Curry Paste (Prik Gaeng Massamun) 33

Shrimp Tom Yum Soup (Tom Yum Goong) 34

Beef Boat Noodle Soup (Kuaytiaw Reua) 37

Coconut Chicken Soup (Tom Kha Gai) 38

Thai Rice Porridge with Pork Meatballs and Coddled Egg (Jok Moo) 40

Thai Chicken Stock 41

NOODLES FOR A LONG LIFE 42

My Classic Pad Thai 45

Lard Nar Noodles (Kuay Teow Lard Nar) 47

Chicken Pad See Ew (Pad See Ew Gai) 48

Pan-Fried Rice Noodles with Chicken and Squid (Kuay Teow Gai Kua) 50

Drunken Noodles (Pad Kee Mow) 51

Crispy Sticky Tamarind Noodles (Mee Krob) 53

Glass Noodle Stir-Fry (Pad Woon Sen) 54

Fresh Rice Noodles (Kuay Teow Sen Yai) 56

KIN KHAO REUYANG?: HAVE YOU EATEN RICE TODAY? 59

Thai Street-Style Chicken Fried Rice (Khao Pad Gai) 61

Shrimp Paste Fried Rice (Khao Khluk Kapi) 62

Street-Style Basil Pork (Krapow Moo Sap) 65

Pineapple Fried Rice (Khao Pad Sapparod) 66

Crispy Rice Salad (Nam Khao Tod) 69

Thai Omelet (Khai Jiao) 73

Stir-Fried Chinese Broccoli with Crispy Pork Belly (Khana Moo Krob) 74

Pandan Sweet Sticky Rice (Khao Neow Moon Bai Toey) 76

Jasmine Rice (Khao Hom Mali) 79

Thai Sticky Rice (Khao Neow) 80

CHICKEN & DUCK: FLAVORFUL FOWL 83

New Thai BBQ Chicken (Gai Yang) 85

Thai Cashew Chicken (Gai Pad Med Mamuang Himaphan) 86

Duck Salad with Lychee (Yum Ped Yang Linchee) 89

New Prik King Chicken (Prik King Gai) 90

Hainan Chicken Rice (Khao Man Gai) 93

Hat Yai Fried Chicken (Gai Taud Hat Yai) 95

Northern Curry Chicken with Noodles (Khao Soi Gai) 97

BEEF & PORK: TIME FOR THE MEAT 98

Garlic Pepper Beef Stir-Fry (Nua Tod Kratiem Prik Thai) 101

Northern Braised Beef Curry Noodles (Khao Soi Neau Toon) 102

Northern Thai Pork and Tomato Chili Dip (Nam Prik Ong) 104

Red Roasted Pork (Moo Dang) 105

Isaan-Style Waterfall Beef (Nam Tok Neau) 107

Thai Sweet Pork (Moo Wan) 108

New Beef Satay (Neau Satay) 109

Thai Braised Beef Short Ribs (Neau Toon) 110

Spicy Basil Stir-Fry (Pad Krapow Neau Sap) 111
Heavenly Beef Jerky (Neau Sawan) 112
Minced Pork Thai Omelet (Khai Jiao Moo Sab) 113
Crispy Pork Belly (Moo Krob) 114
Northern Thai Sausage (Sai Ua) 117

SEAFOOD: OCEAN & RIVER TREASURES 121

Thai Shrimp Cakes (Tod Mun Goong) 123
Clams in Roasted Chili Sauce (Hoy Lai Pad Prik Pao) 124
Crispy Catfish Raft Salad with Green Mango (Yum Pla Duk Foo) 127
Deep-Fried Trout with Green Mango Slaw (Pla Taud Mamuang Yum) 129
Fried Tilapia with Three-Flavor Sauce (Pla Tub Tim Thod Sam Rod) 130
Steamed Mussels with Thai Herbs in Spicy Broth (Hoy Malaengphoo Nung) 133

APPS & SMALL PLATES TO SHARE 134

Thai Crispy Spring Rolls (Popia Taud) 137
Grilled Pork Sticks (Moo Ping) 138
Fried Wontons (Keow Taud) 139
Stuffed Chicken Wings, aka Angel Wings (Peek Gai Yat Sai) 140
Roti Bread 143
Isaan Chicken Laarb (Laap Gai Isaan) 146
Chicken Satay (Satay Gai) 149
Thai-Style Steamed Dumplings (Kanom Jeeb) 150
Thai Savory Bites (Miang Kham) 151
Fried Thai Fish Cake (Tod Mun Pla) 152
Savory Pork Jerky (Moo Dat Diow) 153

SALADS & UMAMI VEGGIES 155

Coconut Mango Salad with Shrimp (Yum Mamuang) 156
Thai Beef Salad (Yum Neua) 157
Papaya Salad (Som Tum Thai) 159
Crispy Morning Glory Salad (Yum Pak Boong) 160
Thai Yum Rice Salad (Khao Yum) 162

Bean Sprouts Stir-Fried with Fried Tofu (Thua Ngok Pad Taohu) 163
Morning Glory on Fire (Pak Boong Fai Dang) 165

PLANT-BASED THAI 167

Spicy Basil Tofu Stir-Fry (Krapow Taohu) 169
Vegan Pad See Ew (Pad See Ew Jay) 170
Vegan Coconut Galanga Soup (Tom Kha Jay) 172
Vegan Yellow Curry (Gang Leung Jay) 173
Vegan Pad Thai (Pad Thai Jay) 175
Vegan Drunken Noodles (Pad Kee Mow Jay) 176
Thai Vegan Fried Rice (Khao Pad Jay) 179
Vegan Tofu Larb (Taohu Lap) 180
Stir-Fried Chinese Broccoli (Pad Khana) 181
Tofu Satay (Taohu Satay) 182
Northern Thai Eggplant and Chili Dip (Nam Prik Noom) 184
Vegan Peanut Sauce (Nam Jim Satay Jay) 185

KANOM WAN: SWEET THAI LIFE 186

Steamed Coconut Custard in Kabocha Squash (Faktong Sangkaya) 191
Sweet Coconut Milk Pancakes (Kanom Krok) 192
Thai Crepes with Pandan Cream (Khanom Tokyo) 195
Coconut Sticky Rice with Mango (Khao Neow Mamuang) 196
Thai Iced Tea (Cha Nom Yen) 199
Thai Iced Coffee (Cafe Yan) 200

SAUCES, DIPS & CONDIMENTS 202

Thai Peanut Sauce (Nam Jim Satay) 204
Grandma's Everything Dipping Sauce 205
Fish Sauce with Chilies (Prik Nam Pla) 205
Homemade Sriracha 206
Ajad Sauce, aka Cucumber Relish for Satay (Nam Jim Ajad) 207
Vinegar with Chilies (Prik Nam Som) 207
Homemade Sweet Chili Sauce (Nam Jim Gai) 208

Acknowledgments 209
About the Authors 210
Index 211

FOREWORD

I'm lucky enough to meet a lot of people around this great country, the world even, who've seen my shows, and I always get a good laugh when I hear the inevitable "Hey, there's that dude who eats the giant burgers!" comments. Look, I love a good burger, but if you really take the opportunity to hunker down and binge on my shows sometime, you'll find that we spend as much or more time exploring the vast and varied culinary landscape of America through the lens of the great ethnic restaurants that are just as much a part of the fabric of our country as your classic burger joints. Moreover, as all of my friends and family are well aware, I'm a junkie for all types of Asian food . . . which leads me here to my buddy, Jet Tila.

Chef Jet brings a little bit of Hollywood to the culinary world. A true product of Los Angeles, Jet was raised in the restaurant kitchens of the "first family" of LA's Thai food scene, and that east-meets-west vibe is very much a part of his culinary point of view. So, while Jet is an absolute machine in the kitchen, the true beauty of what he does is in bridging the gap between the culinarily exotic and what one feels can be cooked at home. Inherently, Thai food is very simple and very complex at the same time. Bright, fresh and uncomplicated techniques can seem daunting when the ingredients are unfamiliar or not necessarily part of our everyday pantry. And when you throw in regional variations and influences from neighbors like China, India, Vietnam, Malaysia and Burma, you've got a whole lot to metabolize in your kitchen. But that's where Chef Jet really shines: as a teacher and ambassador. When Jet cooks in my home kitchen, let me tell you, school is in session, and every meal becomes a learning experience and a true revelation.

In *101 Thai Dishes You Need to Cook Before You Die*, Jet does for the home cook what he also does for me. This book will teach you not just how to overcome the fear factor of tackling Thai cuisine, but it'll also give you a true field guide for what to explore when you go out to eat. His Gold Standards are a genius way to give you both a solid starting point for your explorations as well as permission to keep your eyes and palate open to variations. Contrary to what you may think, you too can cook Thai food, and Jet will show you how. With all of that said, I just wish this was 1,001 recipes because I can't get enough.

INTRODUCTION

I love teaching more than anything. Of course, I love cooking and creating sensory experiences, but the truth is I love teaching more! It brings me joy to create a recipe, have someone cook it and have the food bring them happiness. Maybe it's because they feel a sense of accomplishment after thinking they could never make a particular recipe. Maybe I've given them the passport into a new world. Maybe it gives them pride to feed their family or loved ones. Whatever the reason, I've had the privilege to share something I know with another person and give them happiness. Cooking empowers, it frees and it's a skill that only gives. It creates community, and I've been blessed to share this with you.

What is a gold standard? I've cooked for hundreds of thousands of people in my career, and my food has touched millions if you include my recipes being prepared for diners in restaurants and institutions, on TV, as frozen meals, in fast casual restaurants, etc.

I think it's very presumptuous to say that my recipes from this book are the best or I alone know what Thai food is and should be. That's preposterous! BUT . . . and there's a huge but: If I don't try to teach, translate and transcribe the recipes from my experiences, grandmothers, grandfathers, parents, uncles, aunts, friends—and the countless chefs, cooks and acquaintances that I have had the privilege to learn from, cook with and hang with—then that knowledge dies. It ceases to have the chance to go forward, to be passed on. The opportunity to give this knowledge ends, and what a tragedy that would be.

Thai, like all cuisines, has variations. Recipes vary by family, geography, the individual and even time. Tastes change and evolve over time. So, the recipes in this book are trying to create gold standards based on my 30 years of cooking, eating, learning, traveling and practicing.

My goal with this book is twofold. First, I want to transcribe and simplify how to make delicious Thai dishes, hopefully 101 of the most loved and craved ones. Second, I hope to open up the world of the HOW. I hope to give you the techniques that transcend Thai food to help in all of your cooking. Along the way, keep me posted and connect with #TeamTila on social media. Tag photos of your dishes with @jettila and #101ThaiDishes. Ask me questions via DM on Instagram. Let's create a community together.

PANTRY BREAKDOWN

In this section, we will go over some ingredients that are very common in the Thai pantry and are used throughout this book. I recommend taking the extra effort to track down the right ingredients via the Internet or chasing them down in a local Asian market in your town. They will help you to achieve the gold standard in flavor.

SOY SAUCE

I could easily write a book just about soy sauce. It is an incredibly confusing ingredient when it comes to shopping at Asian markets because there are literally dozens of choices on the shelf. To keep things very simple, let's talk about the ones used in this book: the three main types of Chinese soy sauces and Thai soybean sauce.

Chinese Soy Sauces

Thai cuisine uses Chinese soy sauces as there's a lot of Chinese influence in Thai food. Most of these soy sauces are created through a process called hydrolyzing (versus brewing). Hydrolyzed soy sauce has a much lighter taste than brewed soy sauces; it can taste almost sweet.

There are three main types that you need to add to your repertoire:

- *Thin or light soy sauce* can be considered an all-purpose soy sauce. This is your go-to soy sauce in recipes in this book or any other Thai or Chinese recipes that don't specify a particular type.

- *Black or dark soy sauce* has some molasses, which cuts a lot of saltiness, but it is still decently salty.

- *Sweet soy sauce* is mostly molasses and is great for adding sweetness and a beautiful rich caramel color to a dish.

My family uses either the Dragonfly brand or the Healthy Boy brand. No brand mentions in this book are endorsements. The recipes were simply written using those brands. This is important to know because if you use these brands, you don't have to worry that the dishes will come out too salty or throw the recipes off the gold standard.

Thai Soybean Sauce

Thai soy sauce is a mild yet richer soy sauce. It's not as salty as Chinese thin soy sauce, and it has additional umami and sweetness that give it a very full flavor. It is usually called Thai soybean sauce in recipes, and that's what you'll find in this cookbook. In my opinion, cooks just needed a way to differentiate Thai soy sauce from Chinese soy sauce.

The two most popular brands are Golden Mountain and Maggi. Most families fall into one of the two camps. They are interchangeable, so feel free to use whichever one you can find more easily. I wrote this book using the Golden Mountain brand. My grandmother loved using the Maggi brand so that's what I grew up with. But as I cooked more and more with Thai chefs, I realized the flavor that we are familiar with in Thai restaurants comes from Golden Mountain sauce. So, I have become a convert to using Golden Mountain sauce.

When shopping for this sauce, you may see that the labels for Maggi or Golden Mountain call it "seasoning sauce." In this book I wrote the ingredient as "Thai soybean sauce," but it's the same thing. Take the extra time and find it at a local Asian market or online if you can't find it in your grocery store—it really makes a difference in the dishes.

So, there you have it. Between soybean sauce and the Chinese soy sauces we've covered, your soy sauce pantry is complete.

OTHER SAUCES, OILS & SEASONING

Coconut Milk

I always use full-fat coconut milk in my cooking (not light or low-fat versions), but a can of Thai coconut milk is really two ingredients in one. When you don't shake the can, you can scoop out the thick creamy top, which I refer to as coconut cream. I use that cream to fry curry pastes, which blooms the herbs and spices. Shaking the can into a consistent, even viscosity makes it an all-purpose coconut milk, which is great for making desserts like sticky rice and mangoes or pandan rolls.

Some brands of Thai coconut milk are full fat without saying so on the can. There are also brands that are labeled coconut cream, which are basically just full fat, so it's very confusing. My rules for buying coconut milk are to buy Thai, stay away from light coconut milks and look for a gold "T" (which is the Thailand trust mark). I'm not trying to be a commercial, but it's one of the few times I look out for specific things.

Cooking Oils

My go-to cooking oil is grapeseed oil. In the Thai kitchen, you basically need an oil that is neutral in flavor but can achieve a very high smoke point. Canola, vegetable, soybean and other oils work just fine. I don't know a single person who could blindly taste and tell you the difference between any of these oils. But the taste of olive oil just throws off the flavor of Asian food, in my opinion. Olive oil also has a lower smoke point with grassy notes that just don't play well with Thai and Asian food. I personally feel that coconut oil also has too strong of a flavor to cook with in the Thai kitchen. We use coconuts for milk and sugar, but virgin, cold-pressed coconut oil is a newer creation that doesn't really taste great in Thai cooking.

Curry Pastes

Many Asian countries make curries. They are each unique to their country of origin. The word "kare" literally translates to a spiced sauce, and each country interprets that slightly differently. Thai curries are made from pastes that are primarily made of herbs and spices, versus Indian curries that are mainly dry spices. Thai curries are more palate-friendly for that reason. Add coconut milk and you have a creamy, savory, balanced curry. Most Thai curries are made with coconut milk as the liquid, although there are some made with stocks or are dry, like a stir-fry. Make sure to buy Thai curry paste.

I think of curry colors—like red, green or yellow—similar to how people grade wine. Red and Panang curries are spicier and more intense, so they pair well with bigger proteins like beef or duck. Green is milder and more herbaceous, which makes it go well with chicken and seafood. Yellow curry is almost always served with chicken, either on or off the bone, as the high amount of turmeric creates a mild sweetness that complements chicken really well.

It's also important to read labels if you are a vegan or vegetarian as most curry pastes are made with shrimp paste. There are a lot of brands that don't contain shrimp paste, though; they may be labeled vegan or not have any indicator on the title.

I think it's important to know how to make curry and I did include some recipes for them (see pages 28 to 33). But, 99% of the time I buy it, as it is an art form to balance the spices, herbs and chilies. Like any other artisanal food product, I leave it to the experts to blend curries. Traditionally, curry pastes are pounded together in a stone mortar, which is romantic but takes forever. When I do choose to make them from scratch, I like using a spice grinder that has a removable top because there are wet ingredients. It also makes it easy to wash and sanitize.

Fish Sauce

Make sure you buy fish sauce that's made in Thailand and has a crystal-clear opacity. There are other types of fish sauce that are cloudy and made from ground fermented fish—make sure not to confuse the two. All clear Thai fish sauce is made from anchovies and really is the core of Thai cooking. Like soy sauce, every culture that makes fish sauce has its own little spin on it. So, buying from the country to match the food is the best way to achieve the gold standard in flavor. In a pinch, I like some Vietnamese fish sauce brands as an alternative. There are great vegan fish sauce brands available now if you are eating a plant-based diet.

Msg

Okay, let's have some real talk. Msg has become a controversial and even politicized ingredient over the years, especially in the United States. But the truth is a lot of us Asian kids grew up eating it daily. Msg stands for monosodium glutamate, and it's a seasoning, usually sold in a granular form like salt, that's used to enhance the flavor of foods. Msg actually occurs naturally in a lot of vegetables. Mushrooms, tomatoes and seaweed all have it. Essentially it is umami, that rich flavor of savoriness. As a seasoning, especially among Asian families, it's used in home cooking and in restaurants. It's simply a part of our daily lives.

Let me be clear. I have never used msg in any restaurants I have ever opened or run in my career. But I have used msg when cooking in the home and for friends and family. I personally don't think it deserves the evil label that it has garnered over the years. The fact is it makes food taste familiar. If you've ever eaten at Asian restaurants, I can promise you that msg has been used in many of your meals. And in recent years, it feels like the public is starting to understand that the science behind msg is not as negative as it has been seen in the past.

Here's the thing. You can take it or leave it, but if I fail to add it or mention it, I'm not being an honest Asian cook. My grandmother used it, my parents used it and I use it at home. This really makes it sound illicit, but the fact is, it helps hit that gold standard of Thai flavors, and I would be remiss if I left it out. That's why you'll see it used in some recipes throughout the book.

The bottom line is, if you are up for it, I encourage you to try it. Do some more research on it if you're not sure. And if you have reactions to it or are not willing to use it, then substitute with Chinese chicken powder or just leave it out.

Oyster Sauce

Although the Chinese created oyster sauce, Thai cooks have adopted it and changed the flavor a little bit. Thai oyster sauce is less salty and is sweeter than its Chinese cousin. It is also thinner. I recommend tracking down a bottle of it when tackling this book. I use Chinese oyster sauce when cooking Chinese dishes and Thai when cooking Thai dishes. If you are plant based, you can substitute a Chinese vegetarian oyster sauce. Thai vegetarian oyster sauce doesn't exist as of the writing of this book.

Roasted Chili Paste aka Chili Paste in Soybean Oil (Nam Prik Pow)

This must-have condiment is more of a relish than a sauce. It is one of the unsung heroes of the Thai pantry and is prominent in dishes like tom yum soup and chili paste stir-fries. It is more savory and sweet than it is spicy. It has a beautiful coating effect for stir-fries.

Sriracha

To be blunt, that bottle of sriracha that has a rooster on it—you know the one—is not authentic. Thailand and the original sriracha companies really botched the opportunity to trademark this sauce. I liken it to products like champagne or hatch chilies: It shouldn't be called "sriracha" if it doesn't come from Sriracha, Thailand. The world has grown accustomed now to the flavor of the rooster sauce, but authentic sriracha has a more balanced flavor. There is a recipe in this book to make the Thai version (page 206), but you can also find real Thai sriracha in markets and on the Internet, and I feel it's worth it to try the authentic sauce.

Yellow Bean Sauce

Thai yellow bean sauce is a semi-fermented soybean sauce. Most soy sauces are made from fully fermented soybeans, which give a deep, pungent saltiness. These yellow, less fermented beans have a milder flavor. This sauce is important for Lard Nar Noodles (Kuay Teow Lard Nar; page 47), Morning Glory on Fire (Pak Boong Fai Dang; page 165) and other recipes.

VEGGIES, HERBS & SPICES

Basil

"Horaphā", as it's called in Thai, is one of two common basil types used in Thai cooking. Also known as sweet basil, it is identifiable by its green leaves and purple stems and flowers. It has an intense anise smell and taste.

Hot basil, called "kaphrao", has a spicy taste more like clove and pepper. It is harder to find in markets and is more delicate. The dish "krapow" is named after this basil but usually substitutes it with sweet basil because of the difficulty in finding hot basil.

I think it's okay to substitute Italian basil if you can't find Thai sweet or hot basil. It's not the same flavor, but it's better than not making the dish at all.

Chili Peppers

Thais generally use two types of chilies most often: the Thai bird (prik-keenu), and the serrano-style chili (prik-cheefa). Thai birds are known for being very spicy and have a sustained burn, whereas serrano chilies are moderately spicy and have a quick-dissipating burn. They are interchangeable, so feel free to use either one based on your preference. There are other types of chilies used in Thailand for pastes and sauces, but these are the two most common for cooking.

Galanga (Kha)

This pungent rhizome has a unique peppery, floral and pine-like flavor. It's often confused with ginger because they look similar, but galanga has a smoother waxy skin and an entirely different flavor, so it cannot be substituted. Sliced into thin pieces for soup stocks or pounded into pastes, it holds its place as one of the "Thai trinity" (along with lemongrass and kaffir lime leaves). Don't bother trying to peel the skin off. Not only does that save you time and effort, the waxy thin skin will not affect the texture of the finished dish.

Kaffir Limes & Leaves

Also known as "makrut" for the lime itself and "bai makrut" for the kaffir lime leaves, these have an intense citrus aroma from the essential oils of both the lime rind and leaf. Both are used to make curry and other cooking pastes. The pulp and juice are not used culinarily, but have cosmetic applications. The actual fruit is very difficult to find outside of Asia, but the leaves are readily available at most Asian markets. You can substitute the leaves in any recipe that calls for the rind. Kaffir lime leaves, along with lemongrass and galanga, freeze very well. The best substitute is using lemongrass rather than lime zest. The essential oil in lemongrass, citronelle, is closer in flavor than lime.

Lemongrass (Takhi)

Native to Southeast Asia and easy to cultivate, lemongrass has an intense citrus flavor that comes from its essential oils. Lemongrass is a foundational herb usually paired with galanga and kaffir lime leaves. It is either pounded into pastes or cut into soup stocks. The citrus aroma perfumes many Thai dishes. Make sure to remove the tough, dry outer leaves and the thick base before using it in dishes.

Roasted Sweet Rice Powder

This is a common condiment in Northern and Northeast Thailand, made simply of browned and ground sweet rice. As a powder, it adds a textural crunch but also thickens sauces and dressings. Find the recipe to make it on page 180.

NOODLES

There's no dispute that noodles were created in China, although the Italians think they have perfected them. So, any noodle dish in Thai cooking is a relative or a fusion of Chinese food. The main types of noodles in Thai food are egg noodles, glass noodles and rice stick noodles. Let's dig into each type.

Egg Noodles

In the Thai kitchen, these are very similar to the same noodles in the Chinese kitchen. Also look for "wonton noodles" on the label, meaning they're made from wonton skins, just sliced very thin. These noodles have a nice chewy bite and work great in soups or dry noodle dishes.

Glass Noodles aka Bean Thread

Glass noodles are made from mung bean starch. Starch is what you're left with when you remove protein from flour. Protein is what creates gluten and makes a noodle chewy. When you make a noodle from starch and cook it, it will gelatinize, turn clear and have a spring-like texture. Thai cooks also use glass noodles for anything you would use a rice stick or egg noodle for, like Pad Thai or noodle soups. Most Thai cooks will soak a dry glass noodle bundle in warm water until they separate and are pliable before cooking.

Rice Stick Noodles

These are noodles for Pad Thai and some other stir-fries. They come from the Chanthaburi area, so look for "Chantaboon" on the label. They are also the noodles used in pho. Make sure you buy the correct width of rice stick for the dish you want to make. For Pad Thai, medium is the best size. A medium rice stick noodle is ¼ to ⅜ inch (6 to 9 mm) wide. I use the same width for pho.

When in an area where fresh rice noodles are hard to get, a good tip is to buy extra-large/XL dry rice stick noodles for dishes such as pad see ew (pages 48 and 170), lard nar (page 47) and Drunken Noodles (pages 51 and 176).

Thai cooks usually soak rice sticks in warm water for about 30 minutes to 1 hour, no matter the preparation. Once soaked they can be kept in the refrigerator in water for 3 to 5 days.

RICE

Recent years have brought new rice types to the market, and although I love red jasmine rice, Jasberry rice and other newer types, I'm going to focus on the core rice staples of Thailand.

Thai table rice is always jasmine rice. "Hom mali" is what it is called in Thailand, literally translated to "aromatic jasmine." Like all white rice, it is the polished form of its namesake. White jasmine rice has the bran polished off and the husk removed. You can find brown jasmine rice in the market but most Thai people prize that fluffy, springy texture and sweet bamboo aroma of white jasmine rice.

Thai sticky rice, also known as sweet rice, is a very glutinous type of rice. It is steamed in bamboo baskets suspended over boiling water. This is also the rice that accompanies mangoes after a bath in coconut syrup. There are black (or purple) varieties that are cooked the same way. You can interchange purple sticky rice with white sticky rice in any of the recipes in this book.

MY OPINION ABOUT WOKS

I get asked about woks daily. Do I need a wok to cook Asian food correctly? Does it make the food taste better? My simple answer is: Nobody needs a wok for Asian food unless you have a wok burner. There's no doubt that woks impart a very specific smoky flavor that can't be duplicated—called wok hey, aka the breath of the wok. That only works if you have the kind of heat that wok burners produce—from 50,000 to 200,000 BTU. When you put an Asian wok on an American burner, you're never going to get that wok hey for a few reasons. First, most woks have round bottoms, and stoves are flat. The lack of contact area reduces heat transfer. Also, even the best home stoves generate only 6,000 to 15,000 BTUs, which isn't enough power to create the sustained heat necessary to achieve the breath of the wok.

My personal recommendation is to use an enameled Dutch oven or a large skillet with high sides. When preheated, the cast iron from the Dutch oven is superior for browning and imparting that smoky flavor. The breath of the wok is a very romantic description of that fine line between searing and burning, and you can accomplish that pretty well with a great enamel cast-iron pan. I also like regular cast iron, steel pans, baking dishes and saucier-type pans. A 9- to 11-inch (23- to 28-cm) pan is ideal for high-heat searing.

CURRIES & SOUPS

BOWLS OF YUM

It's believed that curries originated in India and the term "kare" translates to a spiced sauce. Thai curries are almost always made from herbs and spices to create a base paste. That paste is usually fried in coconut or vegetable oil then extended into a sauce with coconut milk, stock or water. Thai curries are delicious and very palate pleasing. You don't have to make curry from scratch—store-bought is great! But, if you are a hardcore cook, I think it's worth making a curry from scratch a few times in your life.

In Thailand and many other Asian countries, soups are almost always eaten as part of a meal with rice and side dishes. Unlike the Western world, you would rarely have a soup by itself. The exception would be morning rice soup or congee. Most Thai soups have that signature "yum"—the balance of salty, savory, sour, spicy and sweet. Occasionally you would have a plain broth. Soups are a vehicle to enjoy proteins like shrimp in Shrimp Tom Yum Soup (Tom Yum Goong; page 34) or chicken in Coconut Chicken Soup (Tom Kha Gai; page 38). Soups are also a way to extract nutrients and flavors from the bones, shells and leftover bits of animals.

I debated whether to break up curry and soups into two different sections, but ultimately I feel they belong together. There will be a longer, more detailed explanation on how to make curries from scratch on pages 28 to 33.

MY FAVORITE NORTHERN CURRY
(Gaeng Hung Lay Moo)

Hung lay is the most popular curry in Northern Thailand and has a crave-worthy sourness from tamarind. You can really see the multiethnic influence from India, Burma and China in the ingredients for this dish. This is my favorite curry by far.

MAKES: 4–6 SERVINGS

1 lb (454 g) pork belly, cut into 1-inch (3-cm) cubes

2 lb (907 g) boneless pork shoulder, cut into 1½-inch (4-cm) cubes

½ cup (168 g) red curry paste

2 tsp (4 g) curry powder

1 tbsp (7 g) garam masala

2 tbsp (30 ml) canola or other high-temperature cooking oil

3 cups (720 ml) chicken stock, or as needed to cover

¾ cup (90 g) roasted peanuts

3-inch (8-cm) piece fresh ginger, cut into matchsticks

30 pickled garlic cloves, peeled (see Pro Tip)

1½ tbsp (21 g) palm sugar or brown sugar

1½ tbsp (23 ml) Thai tamarind concentrate

2 tbsp (30 ml) fish sauce

2 tbsp (30 ml) light soy sauce

2 tbsp (30 ml) black soy sauce

⅓ cup (80 ml) pickled garlic juice

In a large bowl, combine the pork belly, pork shoulder, red curry paste, curry powder and garam masala. Massage together for about a minute to work the marinade into the pork. Cover and let marinate in the fridge for 4 hours or overnight.

When ready to cook, heat an 8-quart (7.6-L) Dutch oven or pot over high heat for about 2 to 3 minutes. Swirl in the oil and fry the pork, turning occasionally, for 6 to 10 minutes until browned on all sides. Pour in the chicken stock to cover by 1 inch (3 cm). Add the peanuts, ginger and pickled garlic cloves. Bring the liquid to a boil, then reduce the heat to a simmer. Cover and simmer, stirring occasionally and scraping the bottom of the pan so nothing sticks, for 1 to 1½ hours, until the pork belly is fork tender and the curry has a nice, thick gravy-like consistency.

To season, stir in the palm sugar, tamarind concentrate, fish sauce, light soy sauce, black soy sauce and pickled garlic juice. Simmer for 5 more minutes, taste and adjust any of the seasonings if you'd like, then serve.

> **Pro Tip:** Thai pickled garlic is a unique ingredient and can be found in Thai grocery stores or on the Internet. It's pickled while young and firm and provides an earthy acidity that cuts through the richness of the pork belly.

PANANG CURRY CHICKEN

(Gaeng Panang Gai)

Panang curry is a type of red curry but has more dried red chilies than fresh, which makes it a milder and slightly smoky curry. Being mild in heat and intensity, Panang is a great curry for just about any protein, from meat to seafood.

MAKES: 4 SERVINGS

4 cups (960 ml) full-fat coconut milk, with 3 tbsp (45 ml) of the thick cream on top separated out

4 tbsp (72 g) Panang curry paste

5 kaffir lime leaves, chiffonade

1 large chicken breast (about 1.8 lb [825 g]), thinly sliced

½ cup (12 g) Thai sweet basil, whole leaves only

½ cup (130 g) sliced bamboo shoots

½ cup (60 g) thinly sliced brown onion

½ cup (75 g) julienned red bell pepper

4 tsp (20 ml) fish sauce

1 tbsp (15 ml) tamarind concentrate

1 tbsp (15 g) white sugar

4 pieces roti bread or homemade Roti Bread (page 143)

¼ cup (35 g) chopped peanuts, for garnish

In a medium saucepan, heat the 3 tablespoons (45 ml) of thick coconut cream over medium heat and stir in the curry paste and lime leaves. Stir-fry for about 30 seconds, until the paste starts to brown.

Stir the remaining coconut milk into the curry paste. Increase the heat to high and bring it to a boil. Allow to boil for 10 to 15 minutes, or until the sauce reduces by about a quarter and coats the back of a spoon.

Reduce the heat to a simmer. Add the chicken, basil leaves, bamboo shoots, onion, bell pepper, fish sauce, tamarind concentrate and sugar. Let the sauce simmer for 10 to 15 minutes, or until the chicken is cooked through.

Cook the bread according to the package directions, or reheat the homemade bread.

Divide the soup among four bowls and sprinkle with the chopped peanuts. Serve with the heated bread.

> **Pro Tip:** Roti bread or paratha can be found in the frozen section of many Asian markets. You can also make homemade roti using my recipe on page 143.

ROAST DUCK RED CURRY

(Gaeng Phed Ped Yang)

This is my favorite Cantonese and Thai fusion dish. The heavy five-spiced, sweet roast duck marries perfectly with the spicy and creamy red curry. You can also substitute the pineapple with canned lychee to make this dish fancy.

MAKES: 4 SERVINGS

6 cups (1.4 L) full-fat coconut milk, divided

4–6 tbsp (84–126 g) red curry paste

6–8 kaffir lime leaves

½ prepared Chinese roast duck, cut into 10–12 pieces (see Pro Tip)

½ cup (12 g) Thai sweet basil leaves

½ cup (60 g) thinly sliced brown onion

2 tsp (10 ml) fish sauce

1 tbsp (15 ml) tamarind concentrate

1 tsp white sugar

½ cup (140 g) large-diced pineapple

6 grape tomatoes

¼ cup (37 g) small-diced red bell pepper

¼ cup (37 g) small-diced green bell pepper

Cooked jasmine rice, for serving

In a medium saucepan, heat 3 tablespoons (45 ml) of the coconut milk over medium heat and stir in the curry paste and lime leaves. Stir-fry for about 30 seconds to 1 minute until the paste starts to brown and the coconut milk starts to separate.

Stir the remaining coconut milk into the curry paste. Increase the heat to high until you reach a full rolling boil. Boil for about 10 minutes or until the liquid has reduced to about a quarter of the original amount and it coats the back of a spoon.

Reduce the heat to a simmer. Add the duck pieces, basil leaves, onion, fish sauce, tamarind concentrate and sugar. Let the mixture simmer for 5 to 10 minutes, until the curry takes on the flavor of the duck and will be thick enough to coat the rice. Stir in the pineapple chunks, grape tomatoes and bell peppers and cook for 2 to 3 minutes, until the bell peppers start to soften. Taste, adjust any of the seasonings and serve over rice.

> **Pro Tip:** You can easily get roast duck at your favorite local Chinese restaurant instead of trying to find a Cantonese BBQ shop.

MASSAMAN BEEF CURRY

(Gaeng Massamun Neau)

This curry is typically served in the south of Thailand, where a lot of the Muslim population does not eat pork. This dish uses a braised beef recipe that's made separate from the curry sauce, but you can stew large beef chunks in the curry, covered, for 2 to 3 hours as well. Like all of the curry recipes in this book, store-bought curry paste will work great.

MAKES: 2 SERVINGS

Braised Beef

1½–2 lb (680–907 g) beef for braising, such as chuck

1 tsp kosher salt

1 tbsp (15 ml) canola or other high-temperature cooking oil

1 stalk lemongrass, cut into 3-inch (8-cm) pieces

5 kaffir lime leaves

1-inch (3-cm) piece galanga, skin on and sliced

3 cloves garlic, smashed

2 cups (480 ml) beef stock or water

Cut the beef into 2-inch (5-cm) chunks and season with the salt. In a large, heavy-bottomed pot, add the oil and place over medium-high heat. Add the beef pieces to the pot and brown on all sides, working in batches if needed to avoid crowding and to get a good sear. Add the lemongrass, kaffir lime leaves, galanga and garlic. Add the stock or water to the height of the beef pieces. Bring the mixture to a boil, then reduce the heat to a simmer for about 45 minutes, covered, or until the beef begins to become tender. Set aside, reserving the cooking liquid.

Heat a wide, deep skillet over medium-high heat for about 1 minute. Stir in 3 to 5 tablespoons (45 to 75 ml) of the thick coconut cream, along with the curry paste, bay leaves and shrimp paste. Stir-fry for about 3 minutes, until the paste starts to brown and stick to the pan and is very fragrant. If it seems dry or starts to sputter, add a little coconut milk to keep it moving. Take care not to burn the paste and spices. The paste should look like it's frying, with oil separating out from the paste.

Curry

4 cups (960 ml) full-fat coconut milk, with 3–5 tbsp (45–75 ml) of the thick cream on top separated out

4 tbsp (54 g) massaman curry paste

3 bay leaves

2 tsp (10 g) shrimp paste

2 tbsp (30 ml) fish sauce

2 tbsp (30 ml) tamarind concentrate

1 tbsp (14 g) palm sugar or brown sugar

1 large russet potato (about 1 lb [454 g]), peeled and cut into 2-inch (5-cm) dice

1 brown onion, cut into 1-inch (3-cm) dice

Cooked jasmine rice, for serving

¼ cup (30 g) roasted peanuts, for garnish

Stir the remaining coconut milk into the curry paste. Scrape the bottom of the pan to release and deglaze anything that may be stuck. Increase the heat to high and bring the sauce to a boil. Allow the mixture to boil, uncovered, for 5 to 10 minutes or until the sauce reduces by about a quarter and coats the back of a spoon.

Reduce the heat to a simmer. Add the cooked beef pieces, fish sauce, tamarind concentrate and sugar. Add the potato pieces and onion. Let simmer, loosely covered, for about 30 minutes, or until the beef and potatoes are tender. Add some of the reserved beef cooking liquid if the curry gets too thick. Taste and adjust any of the seasonings (fish sauce, tamarind concentrate and sugar) if you'd like and discard the bay leaves. Serve with steamed jasmine rice and garnish with the peanuts.

CURRY PASTES FROM SCRATCH

Traditionally, Thai curry pastes are pounded together in a stone mortar, which takes forever, so I like to utilize modern machines. I start the initial breakdown of rough ingredients like lemongrass, garlic and galanga in a small 1-quart (960-ml) food processor to coarsely chop the ingredients into a rough uniform paste. Then I transfer smaller portions to a blade spice grinder with a removable top (rather than the type with a bowl built in) because you will need to add liquids like fish sauce, water or oil to help get a smooth consistency.

See the following pages for the ingredient lists for each paste. Make sure to check and carefully measure each blend's ingredients accurately as the ratios determine which pastes they are. The method for all is the same.

My favorite way to reconstitute dried chilies is to heat a saucepan large enough to soak the chilies over low heat for about 1 minute. Once hot, add the chilies to the dry saucepan and stir, toasting the chilies to bring out the flavor for 30 seconds to 1 minute. You should start to smell the sweet, smoky aromas of the chilies. Add enough water to cover and immediately turn off the heat. Let the chilies steep for 15 to 30 minutes, until they soften. You should be able to pull the stems off with very little effort; that's when it's time to pull them out of the water. Tear the chilies open to pull out the seeds and remove the stem. Pat the chilies dry and roughly chop them.

I never remove the seeds from fresh chilies. Just cut off the stems and roughly chop them before adding to the food processor.

For the dry whole spices, I like to toast them in a dry hot pan for 30 seconds to 1 minute until fragrant, then pop them into the spice grinder alone and grind until they are very fine. You can also choose to use preground spices.

Herbs like galanga, kaffir lime leaves and lemongrass should be chopped as much as is comfortable with a knife. This will help expedite the grinding.

Once the above ingredients are prepped, they can all go into the food processor together. Pulse in 1- to 2-second increments until a rough, even paste forms. This can take up to 2 to 3 minutes of pulsing. You shouldn't be able to distinguish any particular ingredient in the fine mash.

Then, working in small batches, transfer the mash into the bowl of the blade spice grinder, never filling the bowl more than three-quarters full. Grind in 2- to 3-second increments until the mash turns into a paste. If needed, you can add a little water, about 1 teaspoon at a time, because it will evaporate when cooked. Continue to grind in batches until all of the paste is smooth and even.

Store what you don't use right away in airtight containers in the fridge for up to 1 week. You can also freeze it in airtight containers for 2 to 3 months.

RED CURRY PASTE (Prik Gaeng Dang)

MAKES: ABOUT 1 CUP (336 G)

3–4 fresh red Fresno or jalapeño chilies, stemmed and finely chopped

4 dried chilies de arbol or Japones chilies, soaked and finely chopped

2 stalks lemongrass, base and 3 inches (8 cm) of the top removed and finely chopped

1-inch (3-cm) piece galanga, skin on and finely chopped

3 cloves garlic, finely chopped

½ cup (80 g) finely chopped shallots

2 tsp (10 g) shrimp paste

2 kaffir lime leaves, finely chopped

¼ tsp ground black pepper

Water, as needed

*In the photo spread on the next two pages, red curry paste is on the right, in the white bowl with gray edging.

GREEN CURRY PASTE (Prik Gaeng Keow)

MAKES: ABOUT 1 CUP (288 G)

4 fresh green serrano chilies

2 stalks lemongrass, base and 3 inches (8 cm) of the top removed and finely chopped

2-inch (5-cm) piece galanga, skin on and finely chopped

3 cloves garlic, finely chopped

2 tsp (10 g) shrimp paste

2 kaffir lime leaves, finely chopped

½ tsp ground coriander

½ tsp ground cumin

½ tsp ground black pepper

¼ cup (10 g) Thai basil leaves, packed, finely chopped

2 tbsp (8 g) cilantro stems, finely chopped

Water, as needed

YELLOW CURRY PASTE (Prik Gaeng Leung)

MAKES: ABOUT 1 CUP (288 G)

2–4 dried guajillo chilies, soaked, seeded and finely chopped

3 cloves garlic

1 stalk lemongrass

2-inch (5-cm) piece galanga, skin on and finely chopped

¼ cup (40 g) finely chopped shallots

1 tsp shrimp paste

2 kaffir lime leaves

¼ tsp ground cumin

1½ tbsp (18 g) turmeric powder

¼ tsp ground cardamom

¼ tsp fennel seed

Water, as needed

PANANG CURRY PASTE (Prik Gaeng Panang)

MAKES: ABOUT 1 CUP (288 G)

4–6 dried chilies de arbol or Japones chilies, soaked, seeded and finely chopped

2 dried guajillo chilies, soaked, seeded and finely chopped

⅓ cup (55 g) finely chopped shallots

2 stalks lemongrass, base and 3 inches (8 cm) of the tops removed and finely

2-inch (5-cm) piece galanga, skin on and finely chopped

3 cloves garlic, peeled and finely chopped

1 tsp shrimp paste

2 kaffir lime leaves, minced

¼ tsp ground cumin

¼ tsp ground coriander

Water, as needed

*In the photo spread on the previous two pages, Panang curry paste is the top left, in the larger white bowl.

MASSAMAN CURRY PASTE

(Prik Gaeng Massamun)

MAKES: ABOUT 1 CUP (216 G)

4 dried chilies de arbol or Japones chilies, soaked, seeded and finely chopped

2 dried guajillo chilies, soaked, seeded and finely chopped

2 tbsp (30 ml) canola oil

1 stalk lemongrass, base and 3 inches (8 cm) of the tops removed and finely chopped

2-inch (5-cm) piece galanga, skin on and finely chopped

3 cloves garlic, peeled and finely chopped

¼ cup (40 g) finely chopped shallots

1 tsp shrimp paste

2 kaffir lime leaves, finely chopped

1 dried bay leaf

2 tsp (10 ml) Thai tamarind concentrate

¼ tsp ground cumin

¼ tsp cinnamon

¼ tsp ground cardamom

¼ tsp nutmeg

1 tbsp (15 g) white sugar

Water, as needed

*In the photo spread on the previous two pages, massaman curry paste is the middle, in the smallest bowl.

SHRIMP TOM YUM SOUP (Tom Yum Goong)

This is probably the most famous Thai soup in the world. "Yum" in Thai translates to the balance point between hot, sour, salty, sweet and savory. This dish is most well known with shrimp but will work great with any protein or vegetables. Chili paste in soybean oil is the hero ingredient here and must be used without substitute.

MAKES: 2 SERVINGS

4 cups (960 ml) Thai Chicken Stock (page 41)

1 stalk lemongrass, tough outer leaves discarded, sliced thinly on the bias

3 kaffir lime leaves, torn

3–5 thin slices galanga

2–4 dried Thai chilies or chilies de arbol, depending on desired heat level (see Pro Tips)

1 tsp granulated Chinese chicken powder

8–10 medium shrimp, either head-on and unpeeled or peeled and deveined (see Pro Tips)

1 (15-oz [425-g]) can whole peeled straw mushrooms, drained and rinsed

4–6 tbsp (60–90 ml) fish sauce

4–6 tbsp (60–90 ml) fresh lime juice

3 tbsp (45 g) chili paste in soybean oil

¼ cup (4 g) cilantro leaves, for garnish

Bring the Thai Chicken Stock, lemongrass, kaffir lime leaves, galanga and dried chilies to a simmer over medium-high heat in a 3-quart (2.8-L) saucepan. When the broth is simmering, add the chicken powder, shrimp and mushrooms and cook for 2 to 3 minutes, or until the shrimp are pink and almost cooked through.

Turn the heat to low, then stir in the fish sauce, lime juice and chili paste. The chili paste is thick like honey and might need some help to break apart and incorporate into the soup. A whisk works great for this.

Taste and adjust the soup. For more salt, add more fish sauce. If you are lacking acid, add more lime juice. Divide the soup between two bowls and garnish with the cilantro leaves.

Pro Tips: I love using head-on and unpeeled shrimp for this soup. It gives another layer of flavor and is just fun when you peel and eat the shrimp and get your fingers super messy.

If you like your soup spicy, substitute the dried chilies with fresh Thai chilies.

BEEF BOAT NOODLE SOUP (Kuaytiaw Reua)

Boat noodles' namesake comes from the little river boats they are served from in the floating markets. Vendors set up complete cooking stations with burners, bowls and all the ingredients set out, while rowing up and down rivers and canals. Beef blood is the special ingredient that gives the soup a rich body. It's available in most Asian markets in the meat department and sometimes in the freezer section.

MAKES: 2 BOWLS, ABOUT 3 QUARTS (2.8 L) OF BROTH

Broth

1 tsp freshly cracked black peppercorns

1 tsp coriander seeds

4 whole star anise

1 (3-inch [8-cm]) stick of cinnamon

1 gallon (3.8 L) water

4 lb (1.8 kg) beef bones (knuckle or marrow bones)

3 cloves garlic, lightly smashed

1 small onion, roughly chopped

½ cup (10 g) packed cilantro leaves and stems

1 tsp kosher salt

1 tbsp (15 g) white sugar

2 tbsp (30 ml) Chinese thin soy sauce

1 tbsp (15 g) msg

2 tbsp (30 ml) fish sauce, plus more to taste

Build

7 oz (200 g) beef (tenderloin or sirloin)

¼ cup (60 ml) fresh beef blood

7 oz (200 g) fresh or dry rice stick noodles

1 cup (125 g) bean sprouts

½ cup (40 g) Thai morning glory (ong choy), cut into 1-inch (3-cm) sections

6–8 Thai or Chinese beef meatballs

2 tbsp (2 g) store-bought fried garlic

¼ cup (5 g) cilantro, roughly chopped (leaves and stems), for garnish

¼ cup (12 g) thinly sliced scallions, for garnish

Heat a medium stock pot over medium heat and allow it to preheat for 1 to 2 minutes. Add the cracked black peppercorns, coriander seeds, star anise and cinnamon to the dry pot and toast the spices, stirring constantly, for about 1 minute or until fragrant.

Pour in the water and raise the heat to high. Just before the water reaches a simmer, add the beef bones, garlic cloves, onion and cilantro. Bring the stock to a boil, then reduce the heat to a simmer. Stir in the salt, sugar, soy sauce, msg and fish sauce. Cover and cook for 1½ hours on a low simmer. Remove the lid, then scoop out all the solids so just the broth liquid is left in the pot.

If making the boat noodle bowls immediately, keep the broth at a simmer over medium heat. If making ahead, store the broth in the fridge then warm it on the stovetop while preparing the bowls.

While the broth is simmering, cut the beef into thin slices, ½ inch (13 mm) thick by 2½ inches (6 cm) wide, and set aside. Start a separate 3-quart (2.8-L) saucepan of boiling water to poach the noodles and vegetables.

To prepare two bowls, place 2 tablespoons (30 ml) of fresh beef blood in each serving bowl. In a colander or noodle basket, add half of the noodles, half of the bean sprouts and half of the morning glory. Submerge the colander/basket with the ingredients in the boiling water, stirring them for about 1 minute until the noodles soften but are still al dente. Shake out the excess water and place them into one of the serving bowls. Top with half of the meatballs, half of the sliced beef and 1 tablespoon (10 g) of the fried garlic on top of the noodles. Repeat for the second bowl.

Bring the broth up to a full boil. Once it's boiling, ladle about 2 cups (480 ml) of the broth into each bowl. The boiling broth will cook the blood and beef slices. Garnish with the chopped cilantro and scallions.

COCONUT CHICKEN SOUP (Tom Kha Gai)

"Kha" is the Thai word for galanga, an herb that resembles ginger but tastes nothing like it. Galanga is very spicy and herbaceous, with a strong pine scent. It's refreshing and the backbone of this delicious soup. There's much debate about chicken breast versus thigh. I personally love chicken thighs, and they would work in any of my recipes. Feel free to play around with the ratio of coconut milk to stock. If you want a creamier soup, up the coconut milk.

MAKES: 1 QUART (960 ML), 2–4 SERVINGS

3 cups (720 ml) Thai Chicken Stock (page 41)

1 stalk lemongrass, tough outer leaves discarded, sliced thinly on the bias

3 kaffir lime leaves, torn, plus more for garnish

3–5 thin slices galanga

2–4 dried Thai chilies or chilies de arbol, depending on desired heat level (see Pro Tip)

1 tsp granulated Chinese chicken powder

6 oz (170 g) boneless, skinless chicken breasts, cut into thin slices

1 (15-oz [425-g]) can whole peeled straw mushrooms, drained and rinsed

5 tbsp (75 ml) fish sauce

3–5 tbsp (45–75 ml) fresh lime juice

1 (14-oz [414-ml]) can full-fat coconut milk

1 tbsp (15 g) chili paste in soybean oil

1 cup (90 g) cabbage, large dice

Cilantro leaves, for garnish

Bring the Thai Chicken Stock, lemongrass, kaffir lime leaves, galanga and dried chilies to a simmer over medium-high heat in a 3-quart (2.8-L) saucepan. When the broth is simmering, add the chicken powder, chicken and mushrooms and simmer for 2 to 3 minutes, or until the chicken is almost cooked through.

Stir in the fish sauce, lime juice, coconut milk and chili paste. Because the chili paste is thick, it works well to use a whisk to help break it apart and incorporate it into the soup. Add the chopped cabbage and cook until just tender, about 1 minute.

Divide the soup among serving bowls and garnish with the cilantro.

Pro Tip: **If you like your soup spicy, substitute the dried chilies with fresh Thai chilies.**

THAI RICE PORRIDGE WITH PORK MEATBALLS AND CODDLED EGG (Jok Moo)

This is a classic Thai breakfast dish—a warm, savory bowl of jasmine rice porridge, pork meatballs and a cracked egg stirred in. It is the way many Thais start their day. Plus, it's a great recipe for using up any leftover jasmine rice.

MAKES: 1.5 QUARTS (1.4 L), 4 SERVINGS

Pork Meatballs

8 oz (226 g) ground pork

1 tsp fish sauce

1 tsp msg

½ tsp white sugar

Heavy pinch white pepper

Rice Porridge

6 cups (1.4 L) chicken stock

1 tsp Chinese chicken powder

3 cups (600 g) cooked jasmine rice

1 tbsp (15 ml) fish sauce

2 tbsp (30 ml) Thai soybean sauce

Pinch kosher salt

Pinch white pepper

4 eggs

Garnish

3 scallions, sliced

½ bunch cilantro

Store-bought fried garlic

1 tbsp (6 g) ginger, fine julienne

To make the pork meatballs, mix all the ingredients in a medium bowl for about 2 minutes, until the meat feels sticky.

To make the rice porridge, bring the chicken stock to a boil and stir in the Chinese chicken powder until dissolved. Scoop the pork mixture into 1-ounce (30-g) balls and drop right into the boiling broth. Cook for a few minutes, until they are firm to the touch, float and are cooked through. Remove the pork meatballs and reserve until ready to serve.

Now, reduce the broth to a medium simmer. Add the cooked rice, bring it back to a simmer, cover and cook for 10 to 15 minutes, until it becomes a porridge but the grains are still separate and identifiable. It should look like light oatmeal. Season with the fish sauce, Thai soybean sauce, salt and white pepper. Taste and adjust seasonings as needed.

To serve, ladle a piping hot portion (about 1¼ cups [300 ml]) into each of the four bowls. Crack a raw egg into each bowl, top with the meatballs and then garnish with scallions, cilantro leaves, fried garlic and ginger threads. The egg will start to coddle and cook as you stir it into the porridge.

THAI CHICKEN STOCK

This recipe is the base stock for the two most well-known Thai soups in the world: Shrimp Tom Yum Soup (Tom Yum Goong; page 34) and Coconut Chicken Soup (Tom Kha Gai; page 38). If you don't feel like making stock from scratch, you can short-cut this method by adding the aromatics to boxed chicken stock or chicken bone broth. It's also a good all-purpose stock for other dishes like Street-Style Basil Pork (Krapow Moo Sap; page 65).

MAKES: 2 QUARTS (1.9 L)

1 chicken carcass or a whole chicken cut into 8 pieces

8 cups (1.9 L) water

3-inch (8-cm) piece galanga, skin on and thinly sliced

2 stalks lemongrass, tough outer leaves discarded, sliced thinly on the bias

2–3 kaffir lime leaves

2 cloves garlic, peeled

1 large shallot, peeled and sliced

2 fresh Thai chilies, split to expose the seeds

Place the chicken carcass or pieces in an 8-quart (7.5-L) stock pot and cover with cold water. Bring the water to a boil and simmer for 5 minutes. Remove the carcass or pieces and rinse under cold running water until the sediment and scum have washed away. Dump out the cooking liquid from the pot and give it a quick rinse. Return the chicken to the pot and cover with 8 cups (1.9 L) of fresh water. Bring the stock to a full rolling boil over high heat, then reduce to a simmer.

Add the galanga, lemongrass, kaffir lime leaves, garlic, shallot and chilies to the pot and allow to simmer. Skim off any foam and fat often, and continue to simmer for about 1½ hours. Skim off any additional fat and strain the stock through a cheesecloth-lined sieve.

If not using this stock immediately, you can hold it in the fridge for about a week, or in the freezer for 6 months.

> **Pro Tip:** The "Thai trinity" of herbs—lemongrass, lime leaves and galanga—can be frozen if you're not going to use them immediately, or if you have unused extras from making a batch of stock. You can also buy them in dry form online.

NOODLES FOR A LONG LIFE

It's amazing to think that all noodles came from China, considering all the variations in types and flavor profiles we now have around the world. Thai noodles get exciting when you bring in ingredients like tamarind, chili paste in soybean oil and Thai basil. The fundamentals for noodle dishes are the same as in China. Perfectly cooking the noodles to make sure they have excellent texture and taste is key. But what differentiates Thai noodles is the range of flavors. Some dishes are reminiscent of their Chinese parent, like Chicken Pad See Ew (Pad See Ew Gai; page 48), but others are evolutionary, like My Classic Pad Thai (page 45) or Drunken Noodles (Pad Kee Mow; page 51).

Noodles are interchangeable in these dishes. One of my favorite ways to eat Pad Thai is with glass noodles. And on the other end of the noodle spectrum, I love using chow mein–style egg noodles for Lard Nar Noodles (Kuay Teow Lard Nar; page 47). I encourage you to experiment and play with different noodles for familiar dishes. I've also added a recipe for making your own fresh rice noodles because they can be hard to find.

MY CLASSIC PAD THAI

This is arguably the most popular Thai dish in the world. Because this dish has been in America for 50 years, there are dozens of versions. To me, the common thread is tamarind, sugar and fish sauce. Everyone gets to the red color a little differently. I like using paprika for great color without heat. But if you want a little chili punch, back up the paprika with 1 to 2 tablespoons (15 to 30 ml) of Thai sriracha. Rice stick noodles also vary in quality. Look for Chantaboon dry rice sticks from Thailand; they are the best.

MAKES: 2 SERVINGS

Noodles

3–4 cups (360–480 g) soaked medium rice stick noodles, or fresh

Pad Thai Sauce

4 tbsp (60 ml) fish sauce

3 tbsp (45 ml) tamarind concentrate

1 tbsp (15 ml) fresh lime juice

1 tbsp (15 ml) unseasoned rice vinegar

4 tbsp (60 g) white sugar

Pad Thai

2 tbsp (30 ml) canola or other high-temperature cooking oil

2 cloves garlic, minced

2 tbsp (15 g) packaged shredded sweetened radish

1 tsp dried shrimp

½ cup (125 g) savory baked tofu, cut into slices

2 eggs

½ cup (70 g) thin strips of chicken breast or thigh

If you're using dry noodles, soak them in a large bowl of warm water for about an hour. The water should be about 90°F (32°C). The noodles will start to absorb water and loosen up. Drain them well, reserving some of the soaking water to adjust the texture later if needed, and set aside. If you're using fresh noodles, you can just open the package and add them to the pan at the appropriate time.

To make the sauce, combine the fish sauce, tamarind concentrate, lime juice, vinegar and sugar in a small bowl. Make sure to stir well until the sugar dissolves. Set aside.

Heat a wok or large skillet over high heat for about 1 minute, until hot. Add the oil and swirl it to coat the pan completely. When you see wisps of white smoke, add the garlic and stir-fry for about 5 seconds. Add the radish, dried shrimp and tofu and stir-fry until they begin to get fragrant, about 1 minute.

Push the ingredients in the wok to one side and let the oil settle in the center of the pan. Crack the eggs into the pan and add the chicken. As the eggs start to fry, just pierce the yolks to let them ooze. Fold the chicken and eggs over, scrape any bits that are starting to stick and cook for about 30 seconds or until the eggs begin to set. Now stir everything together to combine it all in the wok.

(continued)

10 large–medium shrimp, peeled and deveined

1 tbsp (7 g) paprika, for color

3 scallions, cut into 3-inch (8-cm) julienne

¼ cup (30 g) chopped dry-roasted unsalted peanuts, divided

1 cup (125 g) bean sprouts, for garnish

Add the fresh shrimp and cook for about 30 seconds, until they just start to turn color and become opaque. Add the soaked (and drained) rice noodles and cook for 2 to 3 minutes, until the noodles become soft. Add the reserved sauce mixture and the paprika and fold together until the paprika evenly colors the noodles and all the liquid is absorbed, about 2 minutes.

Place the scallions in the center of the noodles, and then spoon some of the noodles over the scallions to cover and let steam for 30 seconds. Stir in 3 tablespoons (24 g) of the peanuts. Transfer to a serving plate and garnish with the bean sprouts and remaining peanuts.

LARD NAR NOODLES (Kuay Teow Lard Nar)

This is a noodle dish smothered in gravy, the cousin to Chicken Pad See Ew (Pad See Ew Gai; page 48). This would be the saucy version and Pad See Ew is considered the dry version. Yellow bean sauce is made with lightly fermented black beans, so it doesn't have the sharp saltiness of black bean sauce or soy sauce. It is the key ingredient to this dish.

MAKES: 2 SERVINGS

4 oz (113 g) flank steak, cut into thin slices

1 tbsp (8 g) cornstarch

½ tsp baking soda

1 tsp Thai soybean sauce

4 cups (480 g) wide fresh rice noodles (store-bought or homemade from page 56), separated

1 tbsp (15 ml) sesame oil

4 tbsp (60 ml) canola or other high-temperature cooking oil, divided

3 tbsp (45 ml) black soy sauce

3 cloves garlic, coarsely chopped

1½ cups (110 g) Chinese broccoli or regular broccoli

2 tbsp (30 ml) yellow bean sauce

2 cups (480 ml) cold chicken stock mixed with 2 tbsp (16 g) cornstarch

1 tbsp (15 ml) fish sauce

1 tbsp (15 ml) oyster sauce

1 tbsp (15 g) white sugar

Pinch white pepper

Marinate the beef by placing it in a small bowl and mixing in the cornstarch, baking soda and Thai soybean sauce. Set aside.

In a large bowl, separate the fresh rice noodles and toss them thoroughly with the sesame oil, 1 tablespoon (15 ml) of the cooking oil and the black soy sauce.

Heat a large skillet or wok over high heat for 1 minute to preheat. Toss the noodles into the hot pan and cook for 1 to 2 minutes, folding constantly. When the noodles are slightly crisp on the edges and fragrant, place them on a large platter.

Return the same pan to high heat and allow it to preheat for another minute. Swirl in the remaining 3 tablespoons (45 ml) of cooking oil to coat the pan. When you see wisps of white smoke, stir in the garlic, marinated beef and broccoli into the pan and stir-fry for about 1 minute, until the beef is evenly seared on the outside.

To build the sauce, stir in the yellow bean sauce, chicken stock–cornstarch mixture, fish sauce, oyster sauce and sugar and bring to a boil while constantly stirring. When the sauce thickens, taste and adjust any of the seasonings if you'd like. It should be thick enough to coat the noodles without soaking through. If the sauce isn't thick enough, you can add a little more cornstarch (mixed with enough stock to make a slurry), about 1 tablespoon (8 g) at a time.

Pour the sauce, beef and vegetables over the noodles and top with a pinch of white pepper.

CHICKEN PAD SEE EW (Pad See Ew Gai)

This is Thailand's version of chow fun noodles. With pillowy noodles and a sweet-savory sauce, it's a simple but very craveable dish. "See ew" translates to "soy sauce," and it's the sticky sweet soy sauce that is the key to this dish. The noodles are hard to come by so I recommend using extra-large dry rice stick noodles if you can't find fresh noodles.

MAKES: 2 SERVINGS

3 tbsp (45 ml) Chinese sweet soy sauce

1 tbsp (15 ml) oyster sauce

2 tbsp (30 ml) fish sauce

2 tsp (10 g) white sugar

3 tbsp (45 ml) canola or other high-temperature cooking oil, divided

½ lb (225 g) chicken breast or thigh, sliced thin

2 cloves garlic, minced

2 eggs

1½ cups (110 g) broccoli florets (see Pro Tip)

4 cups (480 g) fresh rice noodles (store-bought or homemade from page 56), separated

½ tsp white pepper

To make the sauce, combine the Chinese sweet soy sauce, oyster sauce, fish sauce and sugar in a small bowl and set it aside.

In a large skillet, heat 2 tablespoons (30 ml) of the oil over high heat for about 1 minute. When you see wisps of white smoke, add the chicken and garlic to the pan and stir-fry for about 1 minute, or until the exterior of the chicken is mostly seared and opaque. Don't be scared to really scrape the bits off the pan before they burn.

Add the remaining 1 tablespoon (15 ml) of oil to the pan and add the eggs. Lightly scramble them until they are just set, about 30 seconds. Add the broccoli, tossing it constantly until it starts to turn dark green, 1 to 2 minutes.

Add the fresh rice noodles and allow them to sear in the pan and trade flavors with all the other ingredients for about 1 minute. Then add the reserved sauce and stir constantly to combine for about 3 minutes, until the noodles soak up the sauce and start to crisp slightly on the edges.

When the chicken is cooked through and the sauce is absorbed, sprinkle with white pepper and combine very well, then serve.

Pro Tip: To slightly precook the broccoli florets quickly, place them in a bowl with about 1 tablespoon (15 ml) of water. Microwave for 90 seconds on high, remove, and you're ready to go. You've taken that raw taste and texture out of the broccoli to that perfect point to add it to the wok. You can also substitute Chinese broccoli and your choice of protein in this recipe.

PAN-FRIED RICE NOODLES WITH CHICKEN AND SQUID (Kuay Teow Gai Kua)

This fresh noodle dish is a mild version of Chicken Pad See Ew (Pad See Ew Gai; page 48). It's a simple, very popular street noodle with squid and chicken added. It's one of my favorites when I want a lighter meal. Most noodle dishes are loaded with sauce and salt, and this one is my go-to when I need a break from heavier foods.

MAKES: 2 SERVINGS

2 tbsp (30 ml) canola or other high-temperature cooking oil

4 oz (113 g) chicken thighs or chicken breast, sliced thin

2 cloves garlic, minced

2 eggs

4 cups (480 g) fresh rice noodles (store-bought or homemade from page 56)

½ cup (100 g) squid

3½ tbsp (53 ml) oyster sauce

1 tbsp (15 ml) soy sauce

2 scallions, sliced on the bias

Pinch white pepper

2 large leaves green-leaf lettuce

In a large skillet, heat the oil over high heat. When you see a wisp of white smoke, add the chicken to the pan and stir-fry for about 1 minute, until seared on the outside but still medium-rare in the middle.

Stir in the garlic and sauté until it's light brown. Crack the eggs into the hot pan and lightly scramble them until they're barely set, about 1 minute. Add the fresh rice noodles and squid right into the still-wet egg and cook for about a minute, until the noodles are coated well. Stir in the oyster sauce and soy sauce and cook until well incorporated and heated through. Taste and adjust any of the seasonings if you'd like. Top with the scallions and white pepper, and give it one final toss to warm the scallions.

Tear the lettuce into bite-sized pieces and place on a large serving plate. Plate the hot noodles on top of the lettuce and serve.

DRUNKEN NOODLES (Pad Kee Mow)

One of the noodle dishes I'm most famous for was an accident. I was opening a prestigious hotel and restaurant in Vegas and needed a noodle dish to fill out the menu. I took a classic Thai drunken noodle and gave it some Chinese technique, and it became the most popular dish in the restaurant's history. Thai Basil is the key to this dish, but feel free to use Italian basil if you can't find the Thai.

MAKES: 2 SERVINGS

Sauce

2 tbsp (30 ml) sweet soy sauce

1 tbsp (15 ml) oyster sauce

1½ tbsp (22 ml) fish sauce

1 tbsp (15 g) white sugar

1 tsp Thai sriracha

1 tsp minced garlic

6–8 Thai basil leaves, cut into a fine chiffonade

Noodles

3 tbsp (45 ml) canola or other high-temperature cooking oil

2–3 cloves garlic, minced

2 eggs

1–2 serrano chilies, thinly sliced

6–8 large shrimp, peeled and deveined

½ medium white onion, sliced

4 cups (480 g) fresh rice noodles (store-bought or homemade from page 56), separated

1 cup (25 g) Thai basil leaves, loosely packed

½ cup (75 g) grape tomatoes, halved

Combine the sauce ingredients in a small bowl and set it aside.

In a large skillet, heat the oil over high heat. When you see a wisp of white smoke, add the garlic and sauté until it's light brown. Add the eggs and serrano chilies and lightly scramble the eggs until they're barely set, about 1 minute. Add the shrimp and onion, folding constantly until the shrimp turn pink, about 1 minute.

Add the fresh rice noodles and reserved sauce and toss to combine for about 3 minutes. Don't be scared to scrape the bits off the bottom before they burn. Cook for 1 minute, until the noodles are cooked and coated well in the sauce. Finish by tossing in the basil and grape tomatoes, allowing them to lend their flavors. Cook for an additional minute and serve hot.

CRISPY STICKY TAMARIND NOODLES (Mee Krob)

"Mee krob" translates literally to "crispy noodles." This dish is more like a sweet treat than a traditional noodle dish, and eats like a sweet, savory noodle haystack. It's an old Thai dish that's been featured in cookbooks for hundreds of years, and it found favor in early Thai restaurants in America because it's so easy to eat. We served it in my family's restaurant for more than 40 years. The key here is to make sure the oil is hot enough to fry the noodles so they're light and airy. Think of the noodle nest under Mongolian beef. The sauce is more like a syrup. Remember, fried foods usually get soggy in water-based sauces, but they stay crisp in sugar-based sauces and syrups.

MAKES: 2 SERVINGS

2–3 qt (1.9–2.8 L) canola or other high-temperature cooking oil to fry noodles, plus 3 tbsp (45 ml) for cooking chicken, divided

4 oz (113 g) dry rice vermicelli noodles

¼ white onion, thinly sliced

1 chicken breast (about 4 oz [113 g]), cut into thin slices

6–8 medium shrimp (about 4 oz [113 g]), peeled and deveined

¼ cup (62 g) savory baked tofu, cut into 1-inch (3-cm) tiles

¼ cup (60 ml) tamarind concentrate

2 tbsp (32 g) tomato paste or ketchup

¼ cup (50 g) white sugar

1 tbsp (15 ml) fish sauce

1 tbsp (8 g) cornstarch mixed with 2 tbsp (30 ml) water to make a slurry

Place a wire rack in a sheet pan. Set aside.

In a large skillet with high sides, heat the 2 to 3 quarts (1.9 to 2.8 L) of oil to 350°F to 375°F (175°C to 190°C). When hot, add the dry rice vermicelli in 1-ounce (28-g) batches. The vermicelli will fry, almost triple in size, and puff up immediately. Turn them over and cook the other side for about 30 seconds until pale yellow and crispy. Drain on the wire rack over the sheet pan. Repeat with the next three batches of vermicelli. You can hold the cooked noodles on a sheet pan until you're ready to serve.

In a wok or separate large skillet, heat 3 tablespoons (45 ml) of oil over high heat for 1 to 2 minutes until it just starts to smoke. Stir in the onion and chicken and cook for 1 to 2 minutes, until the chicken is seared on the outside but not yet cooked all the way through, and the onions are translucent and light brown.

Add the shrimp and tofu and continue to stir-fry for about 1 minute, until the shrimp have cooked a little but not all the way through. Now push the contents of the wok up against one side to create a hotspot mid-pan to build the tamarind sauce.

Pour in the tamarind concentrate, tomato paste, sugar and fish sauce. Stir as the sauce comes to a boil and cook for about 30 seconds, or until the sugar dissolves. Add the cornstarch slurry. Constantly stir the sauce as it boils and thickens.

Reduce the heat to low and fold in the noodles, about half at a time, gently folding the noodles together with the sauce and other ingredients in the wok. It will feel like too many noodles for the sauce, but it will eventually come together into a sweet, delicious, sticky pile of noodles. Serve and eat immediately.

GLASS NOODLE STIR-FRY (Pad Woon Sen)

Mung bean noodles, aka glass noodles, are a great addition to a cook's repertoire. They're light, bouncy and create some variety in your Thai cooking. This is a classic street food dish that provides your starch, veg and protein all on one delicious plate.

MAKES: 2 SERVINGS

1 (2.8-oz [80-g]) package dry vermicelli bean thread noodles

3 tbsp (45 ml) canola or other high-temperature cooking oil

2–3 cloves garlic, chopped

4 oz (113 g) chicken thighs, sliced thin

2 eggs

½ small white onion, halved and sliced with the grain (Lyonnaise)

½ cup (60 g) sliced Chinese celery or American celery tops (1-inch [3-cm] lengths)

½ cup (45 g) large-diced green cabbage

2 tbsp (30 ml) oyster sauce

2 tbsp (30 ml) Thai soybean sauce

2 tsp (10 g) white sugar

1 Roma tomato, cut into 6 wedges

2 scallions, sliced on the bias

4 sprigs cilantro, roughly chopped

Large pinch white pepper

In a large bowl, soak the glass noodles in room-temperature water for about 10 minutes, until they soften and are pliable. Drain well, then, using scissors, cut them into 6-inch (15-cm) lengths.

In a large sauté pan, heat the oil over high heat. When you see a wisp of white smoke, add the garlic and chicken. Stir-fry for about 1 minute until the chicken is seared on the outside but still medium-rare.

Crack the eggs into the pan, break the yolks slightly and cook until they start to set, about 30 seconds. While the eggs are still wet, stir in the noodles and stir-fry to combine all the ingredients for about 30 seconds, until the eggs are set but the noodles are still firm.

Stir in the onion, celery and cabbage and stir-fry for about 30 seconds until the vegetables start to soften and mix with the noodles. Immediately add the oyster sauce, soybean sauce and sugar and stir-fry for another 30 seconds until the sauce coats the noodles.

Finish the noodles by adding the tomato, scallions, cilantro and white pepper. Stir-fry for an additional 30 seconds to a minute, until the tomatoes become slightly soft. Taste and adjust any of the seasonings if you'd like. Serve immediately.

FRESH RICE NOODLES (Kuay Teow Sen Yai)

Fresh flat rice noodles are made and delivered the same day to Thai and Asian markets. They harden and go stale within about 48 hours, which makes them very hard to find and to keep. Luckily, they are very easy to make at home and have a great texture when freshly made. These noodles will keep outside of the fridge, covered, for about 2 days.

MAKES: ABOUT 21 OUNCES (600 G) OF NOODLES, ABOUT 5 CUPS ONCE SEPARATED

2 cups (316 g) rice flour

3 tbsp (24 g) tapioca starch (or cornstarch)

½ tsp kosher salt

2 cups (480 ml) water

1 tsp canola or other high-temperature cooking oil, plus more for brushing

Add the rice flour, tapioca starch, salt and water to a mixing bowl. Whisk until the flour, starch and salt dissolve. Add the oil and strain the liquid through a fine-mesh strainer into another bowl. Cover the liquid and let it rest for 30 minutes.

While the mixture is resting, gather a wok and two flat-bottomed pans that fit comfortably inside of it. If you don't have a wok, use a large, deep cooking vessel with a wide opening and a lid. Fill the wok with water and bring it to a boil. (You might need to add more water throughout the cooking process. The goal is to have the pan float on top of the boiling water.)

Brush a light coating of oil on the bottom of the flat-bottomed pan, put the pan on top of the boiling water, and add ¼ cup (60 ml) of the rice liquid to the pan. Tilt it a little so the rice liquid covers the bottom of the pan.

Now, cover with the wok or pot lid and cook over high heat for 3 minutes. If your flat-bottomed pan has a thicker bottom, such as Pyrex, increase the cooking time to 5 or 7 minutes. While it's cooking, brush the second pan lightly with oil.

After 5 minutes, remove the lid, take out the first pan, and set it aside. Place the oiled second pan on top of the water in the wok. Add ¼ cup (60 ml) of the rice mixture. Tilt it a little so the rice liquid evenly covers the bottom, cover with the lid, and let cook.

While it's cooking, attend to the first pan. Brush a cutting board with a thin layer of oil to prevent sticking. Use a rubber spatula to loosen all sides of the sheet of noodle, and slowly lift it up and off the pan. Lay it flat on the cutting board and brush it with more oil. By now, your second pan is probably ready to come out of the wok. Brush the first noodle sheet with a thin layer of oil, then layer the second sheet on top.

Brush the bottom of the first pan with some more oil and get ready to make your third batch. Depending on what pans you are using, you can adjust the amount of batter to make the noodles thicker or thinner as you wish. Repeat the above steps until all of the noodle batter is gone. Don't forget to brush oil between the layers of noodle sheets to prevent sticking.

When all the noodle sheets are made, cut them into ⅓-inch (10-mm) strips, but feel free to cut them in whatever sizes and shapes you like. Then, toss the noodles, loosening each layer to separate them. Now the rice noodles are ready to be used!

Store the noodles, covered, outside the fridge for up to 2 days. If you intend to store them longer, wrap them tightly and store in the fridge for up to 1 week. They might harden slightly, but they should bounce back nicely once heated. Enjoy your homemade noodles!

Pro Tip: If you can't find rice flour, place 2 cups (390 g) of dry white rice in a blender and blend on high for about 1 minute. Strain through a sieve and you've just made rice flour.

KIN KHAO REUYANG?

HAVE YOU EATEN RICE TODAY?

Thais take rice as seriously as any other Asian culture. Instead of saying, "Hello," you would ask, "Kin khao reuyang," or "Have you eaten rice today?" The rice bowl is a metaphor for your family and business. Rice is a very big deal!

Jasmine rice and Thai sticky rice are cultivated and then exported around the world. Thai rice is considered the gold standard. So, the most important first step in cooking Thai food is cooking rice perfectly. A cook can spend many years trying to understand residual moisture, hydration, time, temperature and all of the other nuances in cooking perfect rice. It's an intimate relationship that every cook has with this precious ingredient.

Turn to pages 79 to 80 for my methods for cooking rice perfectly every time. This will be your base for so many dishes. Wherever you are in your culinary rice journey, allow me to guide you through some delicious possibilities. Let's dig in.

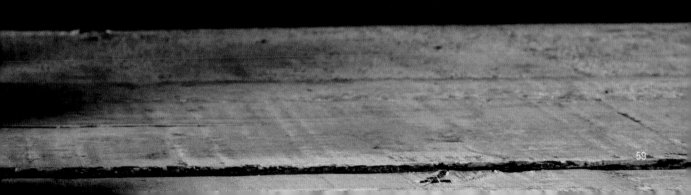

THAI STREET–STYLE CHICKEN FRIED RICE (Khao Pad Gai)

It's undeniable that fried rice originated in China, but it's fascinating to track the evolution and variations of it in each country it traveled through. Even in China it can vary immensely. The hallmarks of Thai fried rice are fish sauce, Chinese broccoli and tomato. They add a very distinct flavor to the Thai version. I think it's more substantial and full of "stuff" than its Hong Kong cousin. Do check out the Cantonese version in my other cookbook. Chinese and Thai fried rice are both delicious and will teach you two very different approaches to fried rice.

MAKES: 4 SERVINGS

3 tbsp (45 ml) canola or other high-temperature cooking oil

5 oz (142 g) boneless skinless chicken breast or thighs, thinly sliced

2 large cloves garlic, minced

2 eggs

½ cup (60 g) sliced brown onion

2 stalks Chinese broccoli, leaves torn large and stalks sliced thin

3 cups (480 g) cooked jasmine rice

1 tsp msg

1 tsp white sugar

1 tbsp (15 ml) fish sauce

1 tsp Thai soybean sauce

Pinch kosher salt

1 medium Roma tomato, cut into 6 pieces lengthwise

½ tsp white pepper

1 scallion, thinly sliced

Heat a heavy-bottomed 9- to 11-inch (23- to 28-cm) pan over high heat for about 1 minute to preheat. Swirl in the oil, making sure to touch every inch of the pan. When you see a wisp of white smoke, stir in the chicken and garlic and stir-fry for 1 to 2 minutes, until the chicken is medium-rare.

Clear some space in the pan by moving the chicken to the edges, leaving the middle bare and ready for the eggs. Crack the eggs into the middle of the pan. Break the yolks and spread the eggs around to cover the bottom of the pan. Cook until they just set, about 20 seconds. Break the egg up and mix it with the chicken.

Stir in the onion and Chinese broccoli and cook for about 30 seconds, until the broccoli wilts and the onion starts to soften. Pour in the rice and carefully smash it flat into the pan, without breaking the grains apart. Continue to fold and smash for about a minute until the rice clumps loosen, combining with the rest of the ingredients and warming it up.

Sprinkle in the msg, sugar, fish sauce, Thai soybean sauce and salt. Keep doing the circular smash-and-fold motion until all of the seasonings are evenly distributed and the rice is hot and toasty, about 1 to 2 minutes. The chicken should be cooked through at this point, and you can check by cutting a piece with your spatula. Toss in the tomato, white pepper and scallions and stir to incorporate and heat for another minute. Enjoy!

SHRIMP PASTE FRIED RICE

(Khao Khluk Kapi)

This is an ornate, beautiful dish made of shrimp paste rice as the starch with a lot of side components. When mixed together, all of the unique flavors, colors and textures make for a fun and delicious meal. I was told it's a dish made by the Mon, an ethnic group that lives in Thailand, Burma and Laos. They were some of the earliest inhabitants of Southeast Asia. I love serving this for guests.

MAKES: 4 SERVINGS

2 tbsp (30 ml) water

2 tbsp (30 g) Thai shrimp paste

1 tbsp (15 ml) fish sauce

1 tbsp (12 g) msg

1 tbsp (15 g) white sugar

3 tbsp (45 ml) canola or other high-temperature cooking oil

2 cloves garlic, finely minced

4 cups (640 g) cooked and chilled jasmine rice

Kosher salt (optional)

Garnishes
Thai Omelet threads (page 73)

Thai Sweet Pork (page 108)

Julienned carrot, cucumber and mango

Thinly sliced shallots, fresh Thai chilies and green beans

Fried dried shrimp

To a small bowl, add the water and the shrimp paste. Use a fork to mix and break up the shrimp paste cake in the water until it forms a smooth paste. Stir in the fish sauce, msg and sugar until well combined. Set aside.

Heat a heavy-bottomed, deep, 9- to 11-inch (23- to 28-cm) skillet or wok over high heat for about 1 minute to preheat. Swirl in the oil, making sure to touch every inch of the pan. When you see a wisp of white smoke, add the garlic and stir-fry for about 30 seconds until light brown and fragrant.

Pour in the rice and carefully smash it flat into the pan without breaking the grains apart. Continue to fold and smash for about a minute until the rice clumps loosen up and combine with the garlic. Stir in the shrimp paste sauce mixture and keep doing the circular smash and fold until all of the seasonings are evenly distributed and the rice is hot and toasty, about 1 to 2 minutes. Taste! If lacking saltiness, add a pinch of salt, stir, then taste again.

To serve, place the shrimp paste fried rice in the center of a large platter and surround it with the garnishes, including omelet threads, sweet pork, carrot, cucumber, mango, shallots, Thai chilies, green beans and fried dried shrimp. I like to use about ½ cup (weight varies) of each garnish for all 4 servings, except the dried shrimp which should be less at about ¼ cup (10 g) total. These amounts can absolutely be tweaked to your taste. Mix everything together and enjoy!

STREET-STYLE BASIL PORK

(Krapow Moo Sap)

Basil pork is as ubiquitous in Thai food as cheeseburgers are in American food. This is a street food version, very different from the one I shared in *101 Asian Dishes*. This one is distinctly Thai with the use of Thai oyster sauce, sweet soy sauce and cut green beans. No bell peppers, and way more gravy and richness. I love this version over hot jasmine rice with a fried runny egg on top.

MAKES: 4 SERVINGS

4 tbsp (60 ml) canola or other high-temperature cooking oil

12 oz (340 g) ground pork (ideally coarse ground)

4 cloves garlic, minced

2–4 fresh Thai chilies, minced

2 cups (200 g) green beans, cut into ¼-inch (6-mm) slices

1 cup (240 ml) chicken stock

2 tbsp (30 ml) sweet soy sauce

1½ tbsp (23 ml) fish sauce

1½ tbsp (23 ml) oyster sauce

2 tsp (9 g) msg

2 cups (48 g) holy or sweet basil leaves, loosely packed

1 tsp white pepper

Cooked jasmine rice, for serving

Fried runny eggs, for serving

Heat a heavy-bottomed 9- to 11-inch (23- to 28-cm) pan over high heat for about 1 minute to preheat. Swirl in the oil, making sure to touch every inch of the pan. When you see wisps of white smoke, add the ground pork and start to press down to spread it across the pan. You want maximum coverage to use the pan's surface area to start the browning. Allow it to cook without stirring or breaking up the meat. After about 1 to 2 minutes, the bottom of the pork will be light to medium brown. Fold the pork over, making sure the raw side sears for another 2 minutes. When the second side is light to medium brown, start breaking the pork into smaller bits. Add the garlic, Thai chilies and chopped beans to the pan and stir-fry for 1 to 2 minutes, until the garlic starts to brown and the beans turn from leathery to bright green.

Stir in the chicken stock and use it to scrape up any delicious bits stuck to the pan. The stock will boil and start to reduce. Reduce the stock by half, stirring occasionally, for 1 to 2 minutes. Stir in the sweet soy sauce, fish sauce, oyster sauce and msg until well incorporated. Let the sauce stay at a boil and continue to reduce until it thickens into a beautiful gravy.

Stir in the basil leaves during the last 30 seconds, but don't let the sauce over-reduce; you want a decent amount of gravy left in the pan. Divide among plates and top with white pepper. Serve with rice and fried eggs.

PINEAPPLE FRIED RICE

(Khao Pad Sapparod)

I love serving this fried rice in a halved pineapple boat, as it always impresses. Thai fried rice usually does not contain egg like the Chinese version does, and the addition of curry powder gives a color and flavor boost. I also like using Chinese sausage for this rice, but you can use chicken breast, thighs or other proteins. If you want some spice, add chili garlic sauce.

MAKES: 4 SERVINGS

1 large pineapple

3 tbsp (45 ml) canola or other high-temperature cooking oil

4-6 cloves garlic, coarsely chopped

3 tbsp (30 g) diced shallots

½ tbsp (3 g) finely chopped fresh ginger

1 cup (140 g) sliced Chinese sausage, chicken breast or protein of choice

4 cups (640 g) cooked and chilled jasmine rice

2-3 tbsp (30-45 ml) fish sauce

3-4 tbsp (45-60 ml) soy sauce

1 tbsp (15 g) white sugar

½ tbsp (3 g) curry powder

2-3 scallions, chopped

Pinch white pepper

3 tbsp (3 g) cilantro leaves, for garnish

Cut the pineapple in half lengthwise. Cut pieces out of the middle and carve out the middle, creating a bowl. Cut about 1 cup (280 g) of the pineapple pieces into a medium dice for making the fried rice. Reserve the rest of the pineapple for another use.

In a large skillet or wok, heat the oil for about a minute. When you see wisps of white smoke, add the garlic, shallots, ginger and Chinese sausage and cook, stirring constantly, until it starts to crisp, about 3 minutes.

Fold in the rice, making sure not to break the rice grains. Gently stir and push down with the flat side of the spatula in small circular motions. This will separate the grains without breaking them. Cook for an additional minute until the rice starts to get hot.

Stir in the fish sauce, soy sauce, sugar and curry powder. Continue to stir for another minute until well combined. Fold in the pineapple and incorporate it well for another 1 to 2 more minutes.

Fold in the scallions and white pepper. Transfer the fried rice to the halved pineapple. Garnish it with some fresh cilantro and serve.

CRISPY RICE SALAD (Nam Khao Tod)

It's almost tough to call this dish a salad as it's made mostly of meat and rice. It's also served at room temperature. Nam sausage is fermented pork skin and sticky rice and is readily available in Thai markets. It adds a tangy meatiness to this salad. You can make this dish without the sausage if you can't get it; just double the ground pork.

MAKES: 4 SERVINGS

Rice Balls

Canola or other high-temperature cooking oil, for frying

4 cups (600 g) cooked jasmine rice, cooled to room temperature

¾ cup (70 g) unsweetened grated coconut

1 egg

3 tbsp (63 g) red curry paste

4 kaffir lime leaves, cut into a fine chiffonade

½ tsp kosher salt

½ tsp msg

Rice Ball Batter

1 egg

½ cup plus 2 tbsp (150 ml) ice-cold club soda or seltzer

1 cup (128 g) cornstarch, divided

¼ cup (31 g) all-purpose flour

Preheat a 6-quart (5.7-L) Dutch oven with 4 inches (10 cm) of oil to 365°F (185°C).

To make the rice balls, combine the cooked rice, coconut, egg, curry paste, kaffir lime leaves, salt and msg in a large bowl. Mix for 2 to 3 minutes, until all the ingredients are well combined. Loosely separate the mixture into eight even loose balls, then squeeze and pack each into a tight ball. Press them flat into ¾-inch (2-cm) discs, then flatten out to an oval about ¾ inch (2 cm) thick.

In a separate medium-sized bowl, make the batter by whisking together the egg and soda water until smooth. Add ½ cup (64 g) of the cornstarch and the flour and stir until a smooth batter forms. In a separate shallow bowl, place the remaining ½ cup (64 g) of cornstarch.

When ready to fry, dredge the rice balls with the cornstarch on all sides, knocking off the excess. Dip each rice ball into the batter, then immediately place them into the hot oil, working in batches to avoid overcrowding. Fry for about 2 minutes on each side until GBD (golden brown and delicious!). Carefully remove the balls from the oil and drain on a wire rack.

Drizzle the remaining batter into the hot oil to make crispy tempura bits for garnishing the salad. Remove the bits from the oil, drain on paper towels and set aside until ready to serve.

(continued)

CRISPY RICE SALAD (Nam Khao Tod) (continued)

Salad

2 tbsp (30 ml) canola or other high-temperature cooking oil

5 oz (142 g) ground pork (ideally coarse ground)

1 clove garlic, minced

½ cup (70 g) thinly sliced prepared nam (pork-skin) sausage

¼ cup (16 g) dried chili de arbol, fried in oil for 30 seconds

1 shallot, thinly sliced

¼ cup (60 ml) fish sauce

¼ cup (50 g) white sugar

¼ cup (60 ml) fresh lime juice

1 tbsp (5 g) Thai chili powder

½ cup (8 g) cilantro, roughly chopped

2 scallions, chopped

¼ cup (30 g) roasted peanuts

To make the salad, preheat a 9- to 11-inch (23- to 28-cm) skillet over medium-high heat for about 2 minutes. Coat the pan with the oil and add the ground pork and garlic. Sauté for about 2 minutes until the pork is mostly cooked. Add the sliced pork-skin sausage and dried chilies and cook for 1 minute, until the pork-skin sausage is heated through, then turn off the heat.

Add the shallot, fish sauce, sugar, lime juice and Thai chili powder and stir until the sugar dissolves. Transfer the contents of the pan to a large bowl. Then, break up the fried rice balls into walnut-sized pieces into the bowl. Toss the crispy rice pieces into the pork and dressing to combine well. Transfer to a large serving platter and garnish with the cilantro, scallions, peanuts and crispy tempura bits.

THAI OMELET (Khai Jiao)

This omelet is simple but has a very special place in everyone's hearts. It's the one dish every Thai cook must know how to make. It's also the one dish you can find at any Thai restaurant or home, any time of day or night. Here I'm sharing the simple classic dish, plus a method to make egg threads to use as a garnish for Shrimp Paste Fried Rice (Khao Khluk Kapi; page 62). If you'd like to try variations, check out the Minced Pork Thai Omelet (Khai Jiao Moo Sab; page 113) for a popular version with ground pork and scallions.

MAKES: ONE 8-INCH (20-CM) OMELET, 2 SERVINGS, OR 1½ CUPS (375 G) OF EGG THREADS

2 eggs

½ tsp fish sauce

½ tsp Thai soybean sauce

½ tsp msg

½ cup (120 ml) canola or other high-temperature cooking oil (3 tbsp [45 ml] if making egg threads)

Pinch white pepper

1 scallion, sliced

Cooked jasmine rice, for serving

> **Pro Tip:** If you're making the regular omelet (not the egg threads), resist the urge to use less oil or you'll end up with a flat, limp omelet.

Crack the eggs in a medium bowl and whisk with a fork for about 30 seconds until the whites and yolks are evenly mixed. Add the fish sauce, seasoning sauce and msg. Continue to whisk for another 30 seconds, until the ingredients are evenly distributed and the eggs are pale yellow and fluffy.

Heat a wok or 8- to 10-inch (20- to 25-cm) skillet over high heat. Add the oil to the pan and heat until it reaches about 375°F (190°C). (See Pro Tip.)

Pour in the egg and immediately reduce the heat to medium. The egg will start to bubble; don't pop the bubbles or push them down. Carefully spoon some of the hot oil over the top of the omelet, to get the center to bubble up and cook evenly.

When the entire bottom is a deep golden brown, carefully turn the omelet over, making sure not to press it down—you want to encourage expansion. Continue to spoon oil over the top until it's evenly deep golden brown and set.

Remove the omelet to a wire rack and allow it to drain for 30 seconds. Sprinkle with white pepper and scallion and serve hot with the rice.

Egg Thread Variation

Heat a wok or 8- to 10-inch (20- to 25-cm) nonstick skillet over medium-high heat. Add only 3 tablespoons (45 ml) of oil to the pan and heat until it reaches about 350°F (175°C).

Pour in the egg and immediately reduce the heat to medium. Spread the egg out over the entire pan and allow it to coagulate and solidify slowly. When the egg is firm enough to flip, turn it over in the pan and cook for an additional minute, until lightly brown and solid. Using a silicone spatula, start with a corner and roll it over on itself. When you have formed a tight roll, transfer it to a cutting board and allow it to cool. Slice into ⅛- to ¼-inch (3- to 6-mm) strips.

STIR-FRIED CHINESE BROCCOLI WITH CRISPY PORK BELLY

(Khana Moo Krob)

This is my favorite dish to eat with jasmine rice for a quick and easy lunch. The rich pork belly is balanced with the slightly sweet and bitter Chinese broccoli and a ton of garlic and chilies. If you can't find Chinese broccoli, you can substitute kale or bok choy. You must add a fried egg on top of this to make it perfect.

MAKES: 2 SERVINGS

1 lb (454 g) Chinese broccoli, leaves cut into 2-inch (5-cm) pieces and stems sliced ½-inch (13-mm) thin on the bias

2 tbsp (30 ml) water

1 tbsp (15 ml) canola or other high-temperature cooking oil

½ lb (226 g) Crispy Pork Belly (page 114), cut into ¾-inch (2-cm) squares

2 large cloves garlic, chopped

1–2 fresh Thai chilies, cut into thin slices

¼ cup (9 g) dried chilies de arbol or Thai chilies

2 tbsp (30 ml) oyster sauce

2 tsp (10 ml) fish sauce

1 tsp white sugar

1 tbsp (8 g) cornstarch mixed with ¼ cup (60 ml) chicken stock (optional)

Dash of white pepper

Place the trimmed and cut Chinese broccoli in a large glass bowl. Add the water, and seal tightly with plastic wrap. Microwave on high for 90 seconds. Remove from the microwave, drain and set aside.

Heat a medium skillet over high heat for about 1 minute. Swirl in the oil. When you see wisps of white smoke, add the pork to the pan and stir-fry for about 1 minute to crisp and heat up the pork belly. BEWARE of spicy smoke in the next step: Stir in the garlic, fresh chilies and dry chilies and sauté until fragrant, about 20 seconds.

Stir in the Chinese broccoli and stir-fry for about 30 seconds, until the edges get smoky and crispy and the broccoli is cooked through. Add the oyster sauce, fish sauce and sugar and stir-fry for about 30 seconds until the ingredients are combined and well coated. If you like a bit of gravy, add the chicken stock and cornstarch mixture and bring to a boil. Taste and adjust any of the seasonings if you'd like. Stir in the white pepper and serve hot.

PANDAN SWEET STICKY RICE

(Khao Neow Moon Bai Toey)

This is a great dessert rice to serve with fruit, coconut custard or even ice cream. Pandan is a sweet-smelling leaf reminiscent of jasmine. You can buy it frozen and blend it with water to extract its flavor. It's also available as a liquid concentrate. Four drops of the concentrate can be substituted for the leaves in this recipe.

MAKES: 4 SERVINGS

Pandan Sticky Rice

1½ cups (280 g) dry Thai sweet rice

1½ cups (360 ml) water

4 pandan leaves, roughly chopped (see Pro Tip)

Salted Coconut Cream Topping

2 cups (480 ml) coconut cream or full-fat coconut milk

1 tbsp (8 g) cornstarch mixed with 1 tbsp (15 ml) water to form a slurry

1 tbsp (16 g) kosher salt

¾ cup (150 g) white sugar

Coconut Syrup

¾ cup (180 ml) full-fat coconut milk

½ cup (100 g) white sugar

1 tsp kosher salt

3 pandan leaves, cut into 1-inch (3-cm) pieces (see Pro Tip)

To make the pandan sticky rice, rinse the rice well with two to three changes of water to remove some of the starch, then place it in a large bowl. Place the water and pandan leaves in a blender and blend on high for about 30 seconds until pureed and very green. Strain the blended green pandan liquid into the bowl with the rice, then add enough water to cover the rice by 3 inches (8 cm). Soak for 3 to 4 hours or overnight in the refrigerator. The rice will absorb the color and aroma of the pandan.

When ready to cook, strain the rice well and allow the water to drain for about 1 minute. You can cook this in a bamboo sticky rice steamer or place it in cheesecloth over a steamer insert pot. Cover and steam for 30 minutes on full steam until the rice is cooked through but still holds its long-grain shape. While the rice is steaming, make the salted coconut cream topping and coconut syrup.

To make the salted coconut cream topping, whisk all the ingredients in a small saucepan until the cornstarch slurry gets worked in and no clumps remain. Place the pot over medium heat for 3 to 4 minutes, until the mixture starts simmering. Keep stirring until the sugar dissolves, 1 to 2 minutes, then turn off the stove. Cool and set aside until ready to serve.

For the coconut syrup, combine the coconut milk, sugar, salt and cut pandan leaves in a small saucepan over medium heat and cook until the coconut mixture reaches a simmer. Stir well until the sugar dissolves, about 5 minutes. Remove from the heat and set aside. Leave it in the pot because you'll have to warm it again to combine with the hot cooked sticky rice.

When the rice is cooked, carefully transfer the hot rice to a large bowl. If the coconut syrup has cooled, heat it up over medium-high heat until the syrup is at 130°F (54°C). It's important that the rice and syrup are hot so the syrup can penetrate the rice.

Pour the hot syrup over the hot rice. Fold a few times with a wooden spoon or silicone spatula to break up the grains and allow the syrup space to coat the rice. Cover the bowl with a plate or plastic wrap and allow it to rest for about 10 minutes. Remove the cover and fold again about eight times, then cut some channels through the rice, really allowing the syrup to soak in. Cover again and let rest at least 15 minutes.

This rice should be held at room temperature if you are going to use it within a few hours. If you're not using it that day, pop it in the fridge. You can microwave the rice for about 2 minutes, stir, then microwave it for an additional 2 minutes if using it from the fridge.

To serve, put a portion of the warm or room temperature rice into a bowl, and drizzle with the salted coconut cream topping.

Pro Tip: Pandan leaves can be found in the freezer section of most Southeast Asian markets. You can also purchase pandan extract on the Internet. Use 3 to 4 drops of pandan concentrate in this recipe.

JASMINE RICE (Khao Hom Mali)

Jasmine rice is the king of rice to Thais. It is unique in the world of white rice and held in high regard for its fragrance, texture and translucence. Most white rice will have the prized grain length but lack flavor, fragrance and a mildly chewy texture.

Brown jasmine rice is the same fragrant rice, but with the bran attached. Nutty in flavor, it has the same aromatic qualities and a slightly chewy mouthfeel.

The only time to adjust your water-to-rice ratio is when the bag says "new crop." Jasmine rice is harvested and released to market once a year. This "new" rice has a higher percentage of residual moisture in the grain, which requires less water and cooks up soft. Reduce your water by 10% to 15% when cooking new-crop rice. Jasmine rice is a 3-to-1 yield, so 1 cup raw will make 3 cups cooked.

MAKES: 2–4 SERVINGS, ABOUT 3 CUPS (475 G)

White Jasmine Rice

1 cup (195 g) Thai long-grain jasmine rice (Hom Mali rice)

1¼ cups (300 ml) water

Brown Jasmine Rice

1 cup (195 g) Thai long-grain brown jasmine rice

1½ cups (360 ml) water

Rice Cooker

1 cup (195 g) Thai long-grain jasmine rice

1 cup (240 ml) water

Add the rice to a fine-mesh strainer and rinse under cold running water while swirling with your fingers. Wash the rice like this for about 30 seconds, and then rinse for about 1 minute. Allow the rice to drain well for 1 to 2 minutes. You can hold the rice in the fridge after washing for up to overnight.

Add the rice to a 2-quart (1.9-L) saucepan, then add the water. Insert your index finger into the pot until you are touching the top of the rice with your fingertip. The water should reach the first knuckle. Set the heat to high and bring the water to a boil. As soon as the water reaches a boil, give the rice a good stir, reduce the heat to a low simmer and cover the pot. After 20 minutes, turn off the burner, remove the pot from the heat and let the pot sit for at least 15 minutes before fluffing with a fork and serving.

If you are using a rice cooker, set the rice cooker to cook. For cookers that just have an on and off button, this process might be as simple as pushing an "on" or "start" button. For fancy machines, select the type of rice and let it work. Cookers that automatically switch from cook to warm might never let the rice rest properly, which means it will keep cooking until it gets mushy. I like to turn off those types of cookers after 30 minutes, fluff, then let the rice keep warm.

Pro Tip: If you can find them, adding six dried butterfly pea flowers will make a beautiful blue-colored rice.

THAI STICKY RICE (Khao Neow)

Most "sticky" rice is short grain, like the kind you eat in sushi. And fragrant rice is usually long grain, like jasmine or basmati. Thai sticky rice is uniquely fragrant, sticky and long grain. It is grown only in the region between Thailand and Vietnam. And it's one of the few rice varieties that you actually steam. It soaks up much of its water during the soaking process. Although we call most rice "steamed rice," it's almost all boiled. A Thai sticky rice steamer is the best tool for cooking sticky rice, and they are cheap to buy.

MAKES: 4 SERVINGS

2 cups (370 g) dry Thai sweet rice

6 cups (1.4 L) water, at room temperature

Add the sticky rice to a medium bowl and cover with the water. Soak the rice for at least 3 hours, preferably overnight.

A Thai bamboo sticky rice steamer is two pieces: an aluminum pot and a bamboo basket. Add 4 cups (960 ml) of water to the pot and place it over high heat.

When ready to cook, drain the rice and transfer it to the bamboo basket of the pot. Give the basket a strong downward tap to seat it well against the bottom of the pot.

Cover with a medium pot lid. Steam for 10 minutes, or until the rice starts to become sticky, then give the rice a flip. To flip, grip the basket by the sides, then jerk it up and slightly forward like you are flipping a pancake.

Let the rice ball steam for another 10 minutes, or until the rice is soft and yields to the touch. Be careful not to get burned by the steam as you're lifting the lid off the basket. Remove from the heat, rest for 10 minutes covered and serve warm.

CHICKEN & DUCK

FLAVORFUL FOWL

The variety of Thai poultry dishes is vast. From the chickens split and grilled on the side of the road on charcoal made from coconut shells, to Chinese-style roast duck in Thai red curry, to duck breast with lychee fruit in salads, the world of Thai poultry cookery is exciting. Choosing between dark meat and white meat is a fight in the Tila house, so feel free to substitute one for the other in any recipe.

NEW THAI BBQ CHICKEN (Gai Yang)

I used to make Thai BBQ chicken the same way forever, and it required a lot of ingredients and time. While working in tech and universities, I realized I needed a quicker way as we were making Thai BBQ chicken for hundreds of people. Thinking about all the herbs and spices that are in curry paste and curry powder, a lightbulb came on. I didn't need to individually source galanga, lemongrass, chili, turmeric and all the other ingredients to make Thai BBQ chicken the old way, because all those ingredients were in curry paste and curry powder. So, Thai BBQ chicken V.2.0 was born and here it is!

MAKES: 8 PIECES OF CHICKEN

1 (3½-lb [1.6-kg]) whole chicken

1 cup (240 ml) full-fat coconut milk

¼ cup (84 g) red curry paste (see Pro Tip)

2 tsp (10 g) minced garlic

1 tbsp (15 g) white sugar

2 tbsp (13 g) curry powder

1 tsp kosher salt

Sweet chili sauce, for dipping

Split the chicken in half. Poke holes in the chicken using a fork and place it in a gallon-size zip-top bag.

Make the marinade by combining the remaining ingredients, except the sweet chili sauce, in a medium bowl. Whisk together until smooth and well combined.

Pour the marinade mixture over the chicken in the bag. Close the bag and massage well to coat it evenly. Make sure the bag is zipped tight then place it in the fridge to marinate for at least 4 hours, or up to overnight.

Preheat the oven to 375°F (190°C) and place a rack just below the middle position. Lay the chicken halves skin-side up on a foil-lined sheet pan and bake for about 45 minutes, or until a thermometer reads 160°F (70°C) in the fleshy part of the thigh. Pull from the oven and rest for at least 10 minutes. You can cut each half into four pieces and serve immediately, or finish on the grill to get some marks and extra flavor. Always serve with sweet chili sauce!

Pro Tip: For those who are allergic to shellfish, a lot of curry pastes contain shrimp, so make sure to check before cooking with them. As a bonus, when you find a brand of curry paste sans shrimp, that paste is almost always vegan for your vegetable curries.

THAI CASHEW CHICKEN
(Gai Pad Med Mamuang Himaphan)

Cashews are grown in southern Thailand and are a huge staple in the Thai diet. This recipe is very different from its Chinese cousin because of its spice and delicious stickiness from the chili paste in soybean oil and black soy sauce.

MAKES: 2 SERVINGS

2 cups (480 ml) canola or other high-temperature cooking oil

½ cup (65 g) raw cashews

6–8 dried Thai chilies

2 cloves garlic, minced

12 oz (340 g) chicken breast or boneless thigh, thinly sliced

½ tsp kosher salt

Pinch white pepper

½ onion, halved, then sliced with the grain (Lyonnaise)

½ red bell pepper, cut into batonnet

½ green bell pepper, cut into batonnet

2 tbsp (30 g) chili paste in soybean oil

2 tbsp (30 ml) oyster sauce

1 tbsp (15 ml) Thai black soy sauce

Cooked jasmine rice, for serving

Add the cooking oil to a medium pan and heat to 350°F (175°C).

Carefully drop the cashews and chilies into the oil and fry for 1 to 2 minutes, until fragrant. The chilies will turn bright red and the cashews should be golden brown. Drain them well and set aside. Discard all but about 2 tablespoons (30 ml) of oil from the pan.

To the same pan, add the garlic and cook until light brown and fragrant, about 30 seconds. Stir in the chicken and stir-fry for about 1 minute, until the outside is seared and it is cooked to about medium, but not yet fully cooked.

Sprinkle with the salt and pepper, stir the onion and bell peppers into the pan and cook until the onion and peppers are light brown and soft, 1 to 2 minutes. Add the chilies and cashews and stir-fry for about 1 more minute until all ingredients are combined and hot.

Pour in the chili paste in soybean oil, oyster sauce and black soy sauce and stir-fry until all the flavors combine and the sauce reduces to a glaze, about 1 minute. Taste and adjust any of the seasonings if you'd like, then serve over a bed of hot rice.

Pro Tip: To cut the peppers into batonnet, this is simply a shape like a French fry, about ¼ inch thick and 4 inches (0.6 x 10 cm) long.

DUCK SALAD WITH LYCHEE
(Yum Ped Yang Linchee)

The combination of duck and lychee fruit is awesome because the sweetness and the acidity of lychee pair perfectly with the richness of duck. Lychee fruit is available all year in cans, but there are certain places where you can get it fresh. I prefer canned lychee for this recipe. This is also a good recipe to utilize leftover Chinese roast duck. Pull the meat apart from the carcass and use it to make this salad.

MAKES: 2 SERVINGS

Duck

2 (2.5–2.8 oz [70–80 g]) duck breasts

Kosher salt and ground black pepper

½ tsp five-spice powder

Dressing

1 clove garlic, finely chopped or pressed

1–2 fresh Thai chilies, thinly sliced

¼ cup (55 g) palm sugar or brown sugar

3 tbsp (45 g) chili paste in soybean oil

½ cup (120 ml) fish sauce

½ cup (120 ml) fresh lime juice

Salad

¼ cup (30 g) thinly sliced red onion (halved then sliced with the grain, also known as Lyonnaise)

½ cup (105 g) lychee, drained

½ English cucumber, halved lengthwise and sliced ¼ inch (6 mm) thick on the bias

1 cup (92 g) mint leaves (leaves picked from the stems)

3½ cups (150 g) romaine hearts, sliced 1 inch (3 cm) wide on the bias

¼ cup (4 g) cilantro leaves

3 scallions, thinly sliced on the bias

¼ cup (20 g) store-bought fried shallots

To make the duck, preheat the oven to 400°F (200°C). Pat each duck breast dry with paper towels. Season the duck on all sides with salt, pepper and five-spice powder. Score the fat on top of the duck in a crosshatch pattern, being careful to score only the fat and not the flesh.

Set an ovenproof nonstick skillet over medium-high heat. Immediately place the duck, skin-side down, into the cold pan. After a few minutes, the fat from the skin will start to render out. Periodically drain the excess fat into a small, heatproof bowl to save it. After 10 to 12 minutes, the skin should be golden brown and crispy, while the meat will still be uncooked.

After the skin reaches a golden brown, flip the duck breasts over, skin-side up. Place the skillet in the oven and cook for 7 to 10 minutes, or until the internal temperature reaches 132°F (56°C). Let the duck breasts rest on a cutting board for 10 minutes before slicing.

Slice the duck on an angle into thin tiles and reserve for the salad.

To make the dressing, in a medium bowl, whisk together all the dressing ingredients until the chili paste and sugar dissolve completely into the dressing. Set aside until ready to serve.

To assemble the salad, in a large bowl, combine the dressing and all the salad ingredients except for cilantro, scallions and fried shallots. Toss to coat well. Taste and adjust any of the seasonings if you'd like. Plate the salad, arrange the sliced duck on top and garnish with cilantro, scallions and fried shallots.

NEW PRIK KING CHICKEN (Prik King Gai)

Prik king is one of the few stir-fries that uses a curry base. It's a perfect Thai-flavored dish, being hot, sour, salty and sweet and balanced with vegetables and protein. This is the chicken version, but it's also common with pork belly. Traditionally it's made with yard-long beans, but I would argue this version with green beans is ubiquitous and more of the gold standard in America. Try it with yard-long beans but if you're not used to them, be prepared for the flavor and texture to be very different, as yard-long beans have a very green, grassy taste.

MAKES: 2 SERVINGS

6 cups (600 g) green beans, trimmed and cut into 2-inch (5-cm) pieces

2–3 tbsp (30–45 ml) canola or other high-temperature cooking oil

4 cloves garlic, minced

2 tbsp (30 g) prik king curry paste

1–2 kaffir lime leaves, cut into a fine chiffonade

8 oz (226 g) chicken breasts or thighs, cut into thin 2-inch (5-cm) strips

3 tbsp (45 ml) fish sauce

2–3 tbsp (30–45 g) white sugar

1 tsp white pepper

½ red bell pepper, cut into batonnet (similar to a French fry, about ¼ inch thick x 4 inches [0.6 x 10 cm] long)

Place the trimmed and cut green beans in a large glass bowl. Add 2 tablespoons (30 ml) of water, and seal tightly with plastic wrap. Microwave on high for 90 seconds to steam them. Remove from the microwave and set aside.

Heat a medium-sized skillet over high heat for about 1 minute. Swirl in the oil. When you see wisps of white smoke, sauté the garlic for about 20 seconds, just until it starts to become light brown.

Stir in the curry paste and lime leaves and stir-fry for about 30 seconds, until the leaves begin to become translucent. Stir in the chicken and sauté for 1 to 2 minutes, until it is cooked to about medium (but not cooked through yet).

Fold in the green beans and cook for another minute, until the chicken is medium-well. Add the fish sauce, sugar and pepper. Fold until thoroughly incorporated. Continue cooking until the chicken is cooked through and the beans are coated with the curry sauce. Add the red bell pepper and cook for about 30 seconds. Serve hot.

HAINAN CHICKEN RICE (Khao Man Gai)

There has always been a cult following for this dish and rightly so. The chicken is supple and flavorful. The rice is rich and garlicky. Overall the dish is simple in concept: a poached chicken, rice pilaf and some sauces. But it's magic when it's cooked well, and this recipe will help you make it perfect.

MAKES: 4 SERVINGS

Chicken

1 (3-lb [1.4-kg]) whole chicken, giblets removed

¼ cup plus 2 tbsp (86 g) kosher salt, divided

2 tbsp (24 g) msg

1 (3-inch [8-cm]) piece fresh ginger, sliced ¼ inch (6 mm) thick

4 scallions

Chili Sauce

¼ cup (60 ml) Chinese chili garlic sauce

1 tbsp (15 g) sugar

1 tbsp (9 g) minced garlic

1 tbsp (6 g) minced fresh ginger

Juice of 1 lime

1 tsp kosher salt

Fermented Soy Dipping Sauce

2 tbsp (30 ml) dark sweet soy sauce

3 tbsp (60 g) Thai fermented soybean paste (see Pro Tip)

1 tbsp (15 ml) Thai soybean sauce

To make the chicken, rinse the chicken under cold water and rub the carcass inside and out with 2 tablespoons (28 g) of the kosher salt to clean it. Rinse the chicken again and pat very dry with paper towels. Cut off the excess skin, chop it finely and reserve it for the rice.

Season the chicken generously with ¼ cup (58 g) of the kosher salt and the msg. Place the ginger slices and the whole scallions inside the cavity of the bird. Place the chicken in a pot just large enough to accommodate the bird and cover completely with cold water. Make sure the bird is totally covered by at least 1 inch (3 cm) of water.

Turn the heat to high and let the water come to a low simmer, about 185°F (85°C). Cook at 185°F (85°C) for about 45 minutes, until the internal temperature reaches 160°F (70°C). Turn off the heat and let the chicken cool in the pot with the liquid while you make your sauces and rice.

To make the chili sauce, in a small bowl, stir the ingredients together until combined. Set aside.

To make the fermented soy dipping sauce, in a small bowl, stir the ingredients together until combined. Set both sauces aside until ready to serve.

(continued)

Ginger Garlic Sauce

1 (1-inch [3-cm]) piece ginger, sliced into very thin tiles

1 clove garlic, peeled

2 scallions, cut into 3-inch (8-cm) pieces

1 tsp kosher salt

3 tbsp (45 ml) canola or other high-temperature cooking oil

Rice

3 tbsp (45 ml) canola or other high-temperature cooking oil

¼ cup (46 g) chopped reserved chicken skin (see directions)

3 cloves garlic, with skin, smashed

2 tbsp (12 g) ginger, peeled and minced

2 cups (360 g) jasmine rice

2½ cups (600 ml) reserved chicken stock, divided

1½ tsp (7 g) kosher salt

1½ tsp (6 g) msg

Garnish

2 pickling or Persian cucumbers, cut into ¼-inch (6-mm) slices

¼ cup (4 g) fresh cilantro leaves

Sliced scallions

To make the ginger garlic sauce, place the ginger, garlic, scallions and salt in a mortar and pound with a pestle until you create a rough paste. Transfer the paste to a sauce bowl, stir in the oil and set aside until ready to serve.

To make the rice, place a 2-quart (1.9-L) stockpot over high heat and preheat it for about 1 minute. Swirl in the oil and the reserved chicken skin, reduce the heat to medium and cook for 3 to 5 minutes, until the chicken skin is brown and the fat has fully rendered. Toss in the garlic and ginger and cook for about 1 minute, until both start to brown. Follow with the rice, stirring to toast it in the fat and aromatics for 1 to 2 minutes until fragrant and toasty.

Turn the heat to high, and ladle in 2 cups (480 ml) of the stock from poaching the chicken, making sure to scoop as much fat off the top as you can. Add the salt and msg and stir to get the rice loose and bathed in stock until it reaches a boil. Cover and simmer for 18 minutes. Turn off the heat and let the rice rest for another 15 to 20 minutes. Fluff the rice before serving.

To serve, slice the chicken and place it over the warm rice on a plate garnished with cucumbers and cilantro. The classic accompaniments are the sauces and a small bowl of the remaining chicken poaching broth with some sliced scallions in it.

Pro Tip: There are a lot of different ways people make the fermented soy dipping sauce for this dish. Pictured is a variation using fermented black beans. In the recipe I call for fermented soybean paste; what you're looking for comes in a bottle and has a thick texture with a light brown color. I like the Healthy Boy Brand Soybean Paste.

HAT YAI FRIED CHICKEN
(Gai Taud Hat Yai)

Fried chicken is universally loved and here's my favorite Thai version. What makes it different is the addition of fried herbs and the spices in the marinade. Dipping options include sweet chili sauce, Thai sriracha or plum sauce. My favorite way to reheat this and all fried chicken is in the air fryer. It brings back all the crispy delicious skin and herby bits.

MAKES: 4 SERVINGS

Chicken

1 small fryer chicken, about 3 lb (1.4 kg), or chicken parts of your choice

Marinade

1 tsp black peppercorns

2 tsp (3 g) white peppercorns

1 tsp cumin seeds

2 tsp (5 g) coriander seeds

½ tsp ground turmeric

1 tbsp (10 g) lemongrass, tough outer leaves discarded, finely minced

4 cloves garlic

2 tbsp (6 g) cilantro stems, chopped

3 tbsp (45 ml) fish sauce

1 tbsp (15 ml) Thai black soy sauce

½ tsp baking soda

¼ cup (60 ml) water

Fried Herbs

5 shallots

Kosher salt

6 kaffir lime leaves, ribs removed

½ cup (12 g) Thai basil leaves

1 stalk lemongrass, tough outer leaves discarded, sliced thinly on the bias

4 dried Thai chilies (optional), stems removed

Break the chicken down into two wings, two legs, two thighs and two breasts. For easier cooking, cut the breast pieces in half, to make a total of ten pieces. Place the pieces in a large bowl. Make some cuts along the leg and thigh bones to expose the flesh to the marinade and make the frying easier later. You can reserve the backbone for later to make chicken stock.

Place the black peppercorns, white peppercorns, cumin seeds and coriander seeds in a spice grinder and pulse until you reach a fine powder, then transfer the powder to a blender. (You can also use the ground versions if needed.) Add the turmeric, lemongrass, garlic, cilantro, fish sauce, Thai black soy sauce, baking soda and water. Blend in 2-second increments until pureed, about 1 minute.

Pour the marinade over the chicken pieces in the bowl and massage it into the chicken for about 2 minutes. Cover with plastic wrap and refrigerate for 2 hours, or overnight.

To make the fried herbs, peel the shallots and slice them thinly, about ⅛ inch (3 mm) thick. Season them with kosher salt and lay them out to dry on paper towels. This will remove excess moisture before frying. While the shallots are drying, prep the kaffir lime leaves, Thai basil, lemongrass and Thai chilies. Set everything out near the stove to make for easier frying.

(continued)

4 cups (960 ml) canola or other high-temperature cooking oil

Batter
¾ cup (120 g) rice flour

¼ cup (32 g) cornstarch

¼ cup (60 ml) water

For Serving
Thai Sticky Rice (page 80)

Sweet chili sauce, Thai sriracha or plum sauce

In a heavy-bottomed pot, preheat the oil to a moderate temperature, about 325°F (165°C). Fry the sliced shallots slowly to dehydrate and crisp them. Stir and turn the shallots over occasionally to fry evenly, about 4 minutes. When the bubbles slow down, use a slotted spoon to take the shallots out just before they turn a nice golden color. They will continue to cook after you remove them, and can become bitter if cooked to a dark color, so be cautious not to overcook them. Remove them to a rack to drain and season lightly with kosher salt.

Have a pan lid in one hand like a shield to protect yourself, then use your other hand to drop in each type of herb one at a time. The basil especially tends to spatter. Fry the herbs until they are crispy, about 90 seconds. Remove to a rack to drain and season lightly with kosher salt.

Increase the oil temperature to 360°F (180°C).

While the oil is coming to temperature, mix the batter ingredients in a bowl; it should be fairly thin, like cream. Pour the batter into the chicken and mix well to coat the chicken pieces thoroughly. When the oil is at temperature, carefully lower a few pieces of chicken at a time into the oil. Cook until golden brown and delicious, and the internal temperature is at least 160°F (70°C), remembering that it will continue to cook a little after removal. Remove to the rack and season with kosher salt. Continue cooking the remaining pieces until all are cooked.

Serve with Thai Sticky Rice, the crispy shallots, herbs, Thai chiles and your choice of sauce.

NORTHERN CURRY CHICKEN WITH NOODLES (Khao Soi Gai)

I often compare this dish to tonkotsu ramen because of its rich aromatic broth, noodles and garnishes. Khao soi is more like a noodle dish than a traditional curry that's eaten over rice. "Khao" is Thai for "rice," but in this dish it is transformed into noodles, and "soi" means to "tear into strips."

MAKES: 4 SERVINGS

Thai Chicken Stock (page 41) prepared using 2 lb (907 g) chicken leg quarters

2 cups (480 ml) canola or other high-temperature cooking oil, for frying

¼ lb (113 g) fresh flat egg noodles, for frying

4 cups (960 ml) full-fat coconut milk, with 3 tbsp (45 ml) of the thick cream on top separated out

2 tbsp (32 g) yellow curry paste

2 tbsp (27 g) massaman curry paste

2 kaffir lime leaves, cut into a fine chiffonade

1 tbsp (15 ml) fish sauce

1 tbsp (15 ml) tamarind concentrate

2 tsp (10 g) white sugar

½ lb (226 g) fresh flat egg noodles, boiled until al dente, rinsed and drained

½ cup (80 g) Chinese pickled mustard greens, drained and sliced thin, for garnish

½ cup (80 g) finely diced shallots, for garnish

2 scallions, sliced on the bias, for garnish

Cilantro leaves, for garnish

Start by making a batch of Thai Chicken Stock according to the recipe on page 41, but using 2 pounds (907 g) of chicken leg quarters instead of the chicken carcass. You'll be using the chicken and 1 cup (240 ml) of the stock for this dish. Reserve the rest of the stock for future use.

While the stock is cooking, make the crispy noodle garnish. Heat about 2 cups (480 ml) of oil in a 2-quart (2-L) saucepan until the oil reaches 360°F (180°C). Prepare a sheet pan with a wire rack or a large plate with paper towels. Loosen the noodles between your fingers and lower them into the oil to fry for about 3 to 4 minutes until golden brown and delicious. Drain well on the wire rack and reserve for garnish.

In a medium saucepan, warm the 3 tablespoons (45 ml) of coconut cream over medium heat and stir in both curry pastes and the lime leaves. Stir-fry this mixture for about 1 minute until the pastes start to deepen in color and are thick and fragrant.

Add the chicken pieces and stir to coat with the paste, about 1 minute. Stir in the remaining coconut milk and 1 cup (240 ml) of the Thai Chicken Stock into the saucepan, being careful to scrape the pan and incorporate anything that was clinging to the bottom. Increase the heat to high to bring to a boil. Allow to boil for about 5 minutes, then reduce the heat to a strong simmer. Simmer for about 10 minutes, until the volume of liquid has evaporated by about a quarter and the liquid coats the back of a wooden spoon. Add the fish sauce, tamarind concentrate and sugar. Taste and adjust any of the seasonings if you'd like.

To serve, separate the boiled noodles among four bowls, and place a chicken leg in each. Ladle about 6 to 8 ounces (180 to 240 ml) of the rich broth over each noodle bowl. Garnish with the crispy noodles, mustard greens, shallots, scallions and cilantro.

BEEF & PORK
TIME FOR THE MEAT

Pork is the more prevalent protein over beef in Thailand in all areas except the south. It's relatively inexpensive and different types of muscles create a lot of variety in these meat dishes. It's hard to imagine Thai food without either of these meats. You can substitute each for one another. Pork shoulder and beef flank are the most useful muscle groups.

Although not heavily consumed compared to other proteins, beef has been part of the Thai diet for a long time. Thais have used cows and water buffalo as beasts of burden and they have often ended up on the plate after their use as a field animal has diminished. In recent years, beef has become ubiquitous in Thailand. In the past it was only for the wealthy and/or only consumed on special occasions.

The two uses of beef will be either stir-fry or grilling. For stir-fry, I like flank, flap or flat iron, as these muscles balance flavor and texture and are not too expensive. For the grill, rib-eye is my absolute favorite, but I also like strip loin, tenderloin or shoulder steaks.

The significant Chinese influence in Thailand also drives the consumption of pork. You'll find it made with every cooking method including stir-fry, charcuterie, braises and grilling.

GARLIC PEPPER BEEF STIR-FRY (Nua Tod Kratiem Prik Thai)

This quick street-food dish is very adaptable. Beef is the classic protein in this dish, but it also works well with chicken, pork or seafood. Prepared deep-fried garlic is a great store-bought ingredient to use anywhere you need crispy garlic.

MAKES: 2 SERVINGS

1 lb (454 g) beef flank steak

1 tsp msg

1 tbsp (15 ml) Thai black soy sauce

2 cloves garlic, minced

2 tbsp (30 ml) canola or other high-temperature cooking oil

2 tbsp (30 ml) oyster sauce

1 tbsp (15 ml) fish sauce

1 tsp ground black pepper

Pinch white pepper

2 tbsp (2 g) store-bought fried garlic

Cooked jasmine rice, for serving

Slice the beef against the grain into thin strips about finger length. Place the beef into a small bowl along with the msg, black soy sauce and minced garlic. Mix to coat the beef well. Let it sit for at least 20 minutes, or as long as overnight in the refrigerator.

Heat a wok or a large skillet over high heat and add the oil. When a wisp of white smoke appears, toss the marinated beef into the pan. Cook for 1 to 2 minutes, continually moving the beef so it browns on all sides but is still rare. Stir in the oyster sauce, fish sauce, black pepper and white pepper. Don't be afraid to scrape any bits off the bottom of the pan before they start to burn.

When the beef is cooked through, stir in the fried garlic and stir for another minute. Serve hot over jasmine rice.

NORTHERN BRAISED BEEF CURRY NOODLES (Khao Soi Neau Toon)

This is hands-down my favorite noodle dish to eat and cook. It comes from my mom's home region of northern Thailand. This dish is very reminiscent of the popular Japanese tonkotsu ramen. The coconut curry is fortified with a very rich broth. "Khao" is the Thai word for rice, in this case rice noodles, and "soi" means "to slice" or "to tear into strips." So this dish was originally made with hand-sliced rice noodle sheets, but the modern version is adapted for thin wheat noodles. Use my Thai Braised Beef Short Ribs recipe on page 110 for the meat in this curry noodle dish. Save the rich stock from that braise for the broth.

MAKES: 4 SERVINGS

2 cups (480 ml) canola or other high-temperature cooking oil

¼ lb (113 g) fresh flat egg noodles,

4 cups (960 ml) full-fat coconut milk, with 3 tbsp (45 ml) of the solid cream on top separated out

2 tbsp (32 g) yellow curry paste

2 tbsp (27 g) massaman curry paste

2 kaffir lime leaves, cut into a fine chiffonade

½ cup (120 ml) beef stock (ideally reserved from the Thai Braised Beef Short Ribs [page 110])

2 tsp (10 ml) fish sauce

1 tbsp (15 ml) tamarind concentrate

1 tsp white sugar

1 lb (454 g) Thai Braised Beef Short Ribs (page 110)

½ lb (226 g) fresh flat egg noodles, boiled until al dente, rinsed and drained

½ cup (80 g) Chinese pickled mustard greens, drained and thinly sliced

½ cup (80 g) finely diced shallots

4 scallions, sliced on the bias

¼ cup (4 g) cilantro leaves

Heat about 2 cups (480 ml) of oil in a 2-quart (2-L) saucepan until the oil reaches 360°F (180°C). Prepare a sheet pan with a wire rack or a large plate with paper towels. Loosen the noodles between your fingers and lower them into the oil to fry for about 3 to 4 minutes until golden brown and delicious. Drain well on the wire rack and reserve for garnish.

In a medium saucepan, heat the 3 tablespoons (45 ml) of the thick coconut cream over high heat for about 1 minute. When the cream starts to sizzle, stir in the curry pastes, similar to building a roux, and add the lime leaves. Stir-fry the pastes for about 1 minute, until they start to thicken, dry out and become fragrant. If the curry starts to sputter, add a small amount of coconut milk to keep the paste moving.

Stir the remaining coconut milk into the curry paste. Increase the heat to high until you reach a full rolling boil. Allow the curry to boil for 5 to 10 minutes, or until it reduces by about a quarter and coats the back of a spoon.

Reduce the heat to a simmer and add the beef stock, fish sauce, tamarind concentrate and sugar. Taste and adjust any of the seasonings if you'd like. Add the short rib meat at the last possible moment before serving; it will take only about a minute for the meat to warm and absorb the luscious curry broth.

Divide the boiled noodles among four bowls. Ladle 6 to 8 ounces (180 to 240 ml) of the curry sauce over each noodle bowl, and make sure each bowl gets a few slices of beef. Garnish with the mustard greens, shallots, scallions and cilantro, finishing with the crispy egg noodles on top.

NORTHERN THAI PORK AND TOMATO CHILI DIP (Nam Prik Ong)

My family comes from the north of Thailand, and this was always a staple dish when my grandmother was making a fancy Northern dinner. There is a method of eating in the North that uses sticky rice as both starch and utensil. You surround the table with spicy, savory and sour pickles and meat dishes. You go in with your sticky rice and have a communal meal. It's a very intimate way to enjoy a meal with your family. This dish is fun because it's kind of like American Sloppy Joes meets incredibly spicy Thai deliciousness. You can also serve it like a fancy crudité.

MAKES: 4 SERVINGS

2 tbsp (30 ml) canola or other high-temperature cooking oil

2–3 cloves garlic, chopped

2 cups (416 g) ground fatty pork, preferably large grind

1 tsp msg

¼ cup (84 g) red curry paste

2 tbsp (32 g) tomato paste

2 fresh red Thai chilies, minced (use serranos if you want a milder heat)

2 cups (400 g) cherry or grape tomatoes, halved

¼ cup (60 ml) chicken stock

2–3 tbsp (30–45 ml) fish sauce

2 tbsp (30 g) white sugar

3 scallions, sliced on the bias

½ cup (8 g) roughly chopped cilantro, for garnish

Thai Sticky Rice (page 80)

1 cup (32 g) pork cracklings or pork rinds

1 English cucumber, sliced into coins

1 carrot, sliced into coins

½ cabbage, leaves separated for dipping (lightly steaming the cabbage is customary and delicious)

Heat the oil in a large deep skillet or wok over high heat for 1 minute, or until the oil just starts to emit white smoke.

Add the chopped garlic, pork and msg, frying and breaking up the pork until the pork is light brown and the garlic is fragrant, about 2 to 3 minutes. If you see a pool of liquid accumulate, strain it out and discard.

Now stir in the curry paste, tomato paste and minced chilies and immediately reduce the heat to medium. Continue smashing the pastes and chilies into the pork, frying until it's fragrant, about 2 minutes. Be careful of the strong spicy fumes with the chilies in the pan; it might act like pepper spray. Add the tomatoes, constantly folding for another minute, until thoroughly combined.

Add the stock, season with the fish sauce and sugar, and bring to a boil. Give it a taste here; if you want it more flavorful, add more fish sauce and sugar. Stir until most of the stock evaporates and the dish becomes fairly thick, 5 to 7 minutes. Taste again and adjust any of the seasonings if you'd like.

Transfer to a bowl, then sprinkle with the scallions and chopped cilantro leaves. Serve with sticky rice, pork rinds, sliced cucumber, carrots and lightly steamed cabbage leaves

RED ROASTED PORK (Moo Dang)

This is the same red roasted pork that you see in Cantonese cuisine. It is a staple protein in the Thai-Chinese kitchen and is used in many noodle and rice dishes. If you want a very bright red color, similar to what you'd find in restaurants, add two to three drops of red food coloring to the marinade. This is a great dish to cook in the air fryer at 350°F (175°C) with a full fan; it mimics the traditional forced air (convection) roasting oven and creates brown crispy edges.

MAKES: 4 SERVINGS

2 tbsp (30 ml) sherry

1 tbsp (6 g) fresh ginger root, minced

⅓ cup (80 ml) Thai oyster sauce

2 tbsp (12 g) five-spice powder

½ cup (120 ml) soy sauce

¼ cup (50 g) white sugar

⅓ cup (80 ml) hoisin sauce

⅓ cup (80 ml) ketchup

2 lb (907 g) pork butt

¼ cup (60 ml) honey

To make the marinade, in a large bowl, stir together the sherry, ginger root, oyster sauce, five-spice powder, soy sauce, white sugar, hoisin sauce and ketchup. Set it aside.

Cut the pork into 3 x 6–inch (8 x 15–cm) strips. Place the strips flat in a shallow baking dish and pour the marinade over them. Let the pork marinate overnight in the refrigerator.

Preheat the oven to 350°F (175°C). Position one rack near the bottom of the oven and the other about 5 inches (13 cm) above it. Place a shallow roasting pan on the bottom rack and add water to the pan until it is about three-quarters full.

Drain the pork, reserving the marinade in a small saucepan. Stir the honey into the marinade until completely combined. Bring to a boil over high heat. When it reaches a boil, remove it from the heat and reserve it for basting and plating.

Carefully place the pork strips on a roasting rack, above the roasting pan, so all sides of the pork strips are exposed to the heat.

Roast the pork for 30 minutes. Baste the pork strips with the honey-marinade mixture. Roast for another 15 minutes and baste again. Roast for 10 minutes longer, or until the pork strips are crisp and golden brown. Remove from the oven and let them cool slightly. To serve, slice the pork into ½-inch (13-mm) strips and smother with the reserved sauce.

ISAAN-STYLE WATERFALL BEEF

(Nam Tok Neau)

Often called waterfall salad, to me it's tough to call this a salad. It's more like a sauced steak with spice and crunch from the rice powder served with fresh herbs. Isaan is the Northeast region of Thailand that borders Laos. Dishes like larb and waterfall salad have sister dishes in Laos and share a lot of common culture. If rib-eye seems too fatty, strip loin is also a great choice for this dish.

MAKES: 2 SERVINGS

Steak

1 lb (454 g) boneless ribeye steak

2 tbsp (30 ml) Thai soybean sauce (substitute thin soy sauce if needed)

1 stalk lemongrass, tough outer stalks discarded, sliced on a very thin bias

1 tsp coarse-ground black pepper

Canola or other high-temperature cooking oil, for rubbing

Salad

2 tsp (10 g) roasted rice powder (see Pro Tip on page 180), plus more for garnish

1½ tbsp (22 ml) fish sauce

1 tbsp (5 g) Thai chili flakes, or to taste

2 tsp (10 g) palm sugar or brown sugar

2 tbsp (30 ml) fresh lime juice

½ tsp msg

½ tsp white pepper

1 shallot, thinly sliced

12 mint leaves

12 sprigs cilantro

1 scallion, sliced on the bias

Steamed Thai Sticky Rice (page 80), for serving

In a zip-top bag, place the steak, the seasoning sauce, sliced lemongrass and black pepper. Seal the bag and massage the steak to distribute the ingredients and coat the steak well. Marinate in the fridge for 1 to 2 hours, or overnight.

When you're ready to cook, remove the steak from the marinade and pat dry with paper towels. Preheat a large cast-iron pan over high heat for 2 to 3 minutes. Rub the steak with a tiny bit of oil on both sides. Sear the steak for 3 to 5 minutes on each side until browned and cooked to your desired doneness. Transfer the steak to a plate to rest for about 5 minutes.

While the steak rests, place all the salad ingredients in a mixing bowl. Slice the steak against the grain into ¼-inch (6-mm) slices, then add it to the bowl. Toss well with the mixture. Taste and adjust any of the seasonings if you'd like. Serve with steamed sticky rice.

THAI SWEET PORK (Moo Wan)

This pork is served as a side dish for Shrimp Paste Fried Rice (Khao Khluk Kapi; page 62) and is often eaten with plain rice or rice porridge. The amount of sugar and the salt that comes from the soy sauces made it a way to preserve pork in the past. Pork shoulder will also work well for this if you don't want too fatty of a cut of pork.

MAKES: 4 SERVINGS

3 tbsp (45 ml) canola or other high-temperature cooking oil

1 lb (454 g) skinless pork belly, sliced very thinly into 1-inch (3-cm) strips

1 shallot, peeled and thinly sliced

¼ cup (55 g) palm sugar or brown sugar

2 tbsp (30 ml) Thai soybean sauce

2 tbsp (30 ml) black soy sauce

1 tbsp (15 ml) fish sauce

½ cup (120 ml) water

Heat a wok or 8- to 10-inch (20- to 25-cm) nonstick skillet over high heat for about 30 seconds to 1 minute. Add the oil to the pan. When you see a wisp of white smoke, stir in the sliced pork. Start the browning process by searing and turning it over every few seconds until all the pork is light brown, 2 to 3 minutes. Stir in the shallot and continue cooking and turning for an additional minute, until the shallot is translucent. When the pork is browned and cooked through, drain off any excess oil or liquid in the pan and discard it.

Bring the pan back to high heat and add the sugar, soybean sauce, black soy sauce, fish sauce and water. Stir until the sauce is well combined and bring it to a boil. Reduce the heat to a simmer, cover and cook until tender, about 15 minutes. Then remove the lid to allow the liquid to reduce into a glaze, about 10 minutes.

Serve as a side to the Shrimp Paste Fried Rice (page 62) or with plain rice.

NEW BEEF SATAY (Neau Satay)

I like this version of satay for its simplicity and readily available ingredients. You can also substitute any beef steak like strip loin, filet mignon or rib-eye for the flank steak. Pair this with the Thai Peanut Sauce (Nam Jim Satay) on page 204.

MAKES: 4 SERVINGS

1 tbsp (6 g) curry powder

1 tbsp (15 g) white sugar

1 tbsp (14 g) kosher salt

½ tbsp (3 g) ground black pepper

1 tsp garlic powder

¼ cup (60 ml) full-fat coconut milk

2 lb (907 g) beef flank steak

20–30 bamboo skewers, soaked in water (see Pro Tip)

Thai Peanut Sauce (page 204), for serving

To make the marinade, combine the curry powder, sugar, salt, pepper and garlic powder in a large bowl. Stir in the coconut milk until it's well combined with the spices. Slice the flank steak against the grain into 1½-inch (4-cm) slices. Add the steak to the marinade, and massage well, coating the beef evenly.

Thread the beef onto the soaked skewers, leaving 1½ to 2 inches (4 to 5 cm) free at the bottom of each skewer. Cover the skewers and let them marinate in the fridge for 4 hours or overnight.

When ready to cook, preheat a grill or stove-top grill pan to high. Grill the skewers until you get grill marks and the beef is cooked through, 3 to 5 minutes on each side. Serve with the peanut sauce.

> **Pro Tip:** Fold aluminum foil into double-thick pieces and wrap around the bottoms of the skewers to protect them from burning on the grill.

THAI BRAISED BEEF SHORT RIBS (Neau Toon)

I always keep cooked short ribs in the freezer for a quick meal or to throw into fried rice, noodle dishes and more. This is actually a classic French recipe for braised beef short ribs. But I had to include it because it serves as the perfect tender and moist beef for a few dishes in the book. Here I've given it a Thai twist with lemongrass, star anise, cilantro and fish sauce. Short ribs are better served a day or two after they are cooked.

MAKES: 4 SERVINGS

½ cup (63 g) all-purpose flour

1 tbsp (15 g) kosher salt

1 tsp cracked pepper

4 lb (1.8 kg) beef short ribs

¼ cup (56 g) unsalted butter, divided

2 shallots, chopped

3 cloves garlic, chopped

½ lb (226 g) onion, cut into large dice

¼ lb (113 g) lemongrass, cut into large dice

¼ lb (113 g) celery, cut into large dice

1 (25-oz [750-ml]) bottle dry red wine

2 bay leaves

3 whole star anise

1 sprig cilantro

¼ cup (60 ml) fish sauce

4 cups (960 ml) beef broth

Preheat the oven to 325°F (165°C).

Combine the flour, salt and pepper in a large bowl. Dredge the beef in the seasoned flour and shake off the excess; set aside. Heat 2 table-spoons (28 g) of the butter in a 4- or 5-quart (3.8- to 4.8-L) Dutch oven over high heat. Brown the short ribs on all sides, about 10 minutes. Transfer the browned short ribs to a plate and set aside.

Melt another 2 tablespoons (28 g) of the butter in the Dutch oven. Stir in the shallots, garlic, onion, lemongrass and celery. Cook and stir until the vegetables have softened, about 10 minutes. Add the wine and reduce it by half. Stir in the bay leaves, star anise, cilantro, fish sauce and beef broth. Place the browned short ribs on top of the vegetables in a single layer, and then bring it to a boil.

Cover it with a tight-fitting lid or aluminum foil, then bake it in the preheated oven until the short ribs are very tender and nearly falling off the bone, 3 to 3½ hours. When the short ribs are tender, strip the meat off the bone with a fork and place in a serving dish. If you're not serving it immediately, cover and keep warm, or store in the fridge or freezer until needed.

SPICY BASIL STIR-FRY (Pad Krapow Neau Sap)

Thai spicy basil is my default order at restaurants when I'm just not sure what to eat because it's delicious, simple and a complete meal when served over rice, especially with a fried egg on top. It's sold in every single Thai restaurant and street stall. The only customization is your choice of meat or seafood. So, feel free to change it up when making this dish.

MAKES: 4 SERVINGS

3 tbsp (45 ml) sweet soy sauce

2 tbsp (30 ml) oyster sauce

4 tbsp (60 ml) fish sauce

2 tbsp (30 g) chili paste in soybean oil

3 tbsp (45 ml) canola or other high-temperature cooking oil

3 cloves garlic, minced

1–3 fresh serrano or Thai chilies, sliced

3 cups (798 g) lean ground beef (ideally freshly ground on a large die)

1 onion, sliced

1 red bell pepper, sliced

1½ cups (48 g) Thai basil leaves, loosely packed

½ tsp white pepper

Cooked jasmine rice, for serving

To make the sauce, combine the sweet soy sauce, oyster sauce, fish sauce and chili paste in soybean oil in a small bowl. Set aside.

Heat a wok or large skillet over high heat and add the oil. When a wisp of white smoke appears, add the garlic and chilies. Cook them until the garlic starts to brown, about 30 seconds.

Stir in the ground beef, flatten it against the pan and cook undisturbed for about 45 seconds. The beef will start to brown. Turn it over once, again press it flat against the pan and cook for another 30 seconds. Break up the meat into gravel-sized pieces. Drain and discard any excess liquid.

Stir in the onion and bell pepper and stir-fry for about 1 minute. Add the reserved sauce and stir to combine the ingredients thoroughly for about 1 minute. Add the Thai basil and stir-fry until the beef is thoroughly cooked and the onions are slightly tender. Finish with the white pepper and serve over hot rice.

HEAVENLY BEEF JERKY (Neau Sawan)

"Neau sawan" literally translates to heavenly beef, and rightly so. Unlike American jerky, this version is sweet, sticky and herbaceous. Coriander is the secret ingredient and is delicious in this jerky. If you have an air fryer, the dehydrator mode is perfect for a quick cook.

MAKES: 4 SERVINGS

3 lb (1.4 kg) beef top sirloin

¾ cup (150 g) white sugar

2 tbsp (13 g) black pepper

5 tbsp (30 g) cumin seed, toasted and ground

5 tbsp (25 g) coriander seed, toasted and ground

3 tbsp (45 ml) fish sauce

3 tbsp (45 ml) oyster sauce

3 tbsp (45 ml) thin soy sauce

1 tbsp (15 ml) Thai soybean sauce

1 tbsp (7 g) toasted sesame seeds

Slice the beef paper thin, into ⅛- to ¼-inch (3- to 6-mm) slices, and place them in a medium bowl. Add the remaining ingredients except for the toasted sesame seeds. Massage the beef with your hands for about 2 to 3 minutes until well coated. Cover and refrigerate for 2 to 4 hours, allowing the marinade to penetrate the beef.

Remove the beef from the marinade and allow it to drain on a wire rack that fits over a parchment-lined cookie sheet. Place the rack and cookie sheet in the fridge for 1 to 2 hours to air dry.

When you're ready to bake, preheat the oven to 170°F (75°C). Discard the parchment paper on the cookie sheet, and replace it with a new sheet. Sprinkle the sesame seeds on top of the beef. Bake for 2 to 3 hours until cooked through, browned and sticky.

> Pro Tip: Frying the beef is also a popular way to cook the jerky. Fry at 350°F (175°C) for 2 to 3 minutes until golden brown and just cooked through.

MINCED PORK THAI OMELET
(Khai Jiao Moo Sab)

This is a quintessential Thai dish eaten by all Thais. It's an aerated seasoned omelet that's deep-fried in oil which gives it density, heft and a unique crispness. It's like a crispy savory eggy cloud that pairs perfectly with warm jasmine rice and sriracha. It's kind of like a Thailand bologna sandwich—we all eat it and it's always satisfying. I have a plain version of Thai Omelet (Khai Jiao) on page 73, and this version is a great variation with pork and scallions.

MAKES: ONE 8-INCH (20-CM) OMELET

2 eggs

2 oz (57 g) ground pork (ideally coarsely ground)

½ tsp fish sauce

½ tsp Thai soybean sauce

½ tsp msg

½ scallion, thinly sliced

½ cup (120 ml) canola or other high-temperature cooking oil (see Pro Tip)

Pinch white pepper

Crack the eggs in a medium bowl and whisk with a fork for about 30 seconds, until the whites and yolks are evenly mixed. Add the pork, fish sauce, soybean sauce, msg and scallion. Continue to whisk for another 30 seconds, until the ingredients are evenly distributed and the eggs are pale yellow and fluffy.

Heat a wok or 8- to 10-inch (20- to 25-cm) skillet over high heat. Add the oil to the pan and heat until it reaches about 375°F (190°C).

Pour in the egg and immediately reduce the heat to medium. The egg will start to bubble; don't pop the bubbles or push them down. Carefully spoon some of the hot oil over the top of the omelet, to get the center to bubble up and cook evenly.

When the entire bottom is a deep golden brown, carefully turn the omelet over, making sure not to press it down—you want to encourage expansion. Continue to spoon oil over the top until it's evenly deep golden brown and set.

Remove the omelet to a wire rack and allow it to drain excess oil for about 30 seconds. Serve hot with a sprinkle of white pepper.

> **Pro Tip:** You're going to have to resist your urge to use less oil or you'll end up with a flat, limp omelet.

CRISPY PORK BELLY (Moo Krob)

This is the crown jewel to many chefs and food aficionados. Taking a tough and fatty pork belly, cooking it with moist heat until tender and then frying it into crispy pieces is truly heaven. You can eat it over rice, add it to noodle dishes and stir-fry it with chili and basil. But no matter how you use it, learning how to make crispy pork belly is a fundamental skill.

MAKES: 2 LBS (907 G)

6 cups (1.4 L) water

5 tbsp (72 g) kosher salt

1 (2–2.5 lb [907 g–1.2 kg]) pork belly, center cut

Canola or other high-temperature cooking oil, for frying

Mix the water and salt in a pot big enough to hold the pork belly. Cut the pork belly into two pieces lengthwise. Soak the pork in the salt solution for 30 minutes at room temperature. Place the pot on the stove, position the pork so it is skin-side down, and bring to a boil. Reduce the heat to a simmer, cover loosely and cook for 1 hour. Check occasionally that the pork is not stuck to the bottom of the pan.

After 1 hour, check the meat side for tenderness with a fork. The fork should be able to pierce the meat, but it won't be falling apart. If you can't pierce the meat, cook for an additional 20 minutes. Turn off the heat, turn the pieces over so the skin is exposed to the air, and let the pork cool down in the liquid. When cool, discard the liquid.

Preheat the oven to 350°F (175°C).

Then Swiss or pierce the skin, which creates pockets for the oil to penetrate the skin to fry and puff it up. Just pierce the skin, don't go too deep. A meat tenderizer tool is best, but a fork or skewers held together with a rubber band will work. Before baking, score the pork on the skin side to pre-mark the cut lines. This will keep the pork from cracking later and will give you perfectly cut strips. Score 1- to 2-inch (3- to 5-cm) sections just through the skin, about ⅛ inch (3 mm) deep.

Bake the pork pieces in the oven for 1 hour. Remove the pork from the oven and allow it to dry, uncovered, in the fridge overnight. The skin should be quite firm, like plastic or resin.

In a large pot, preheat enough oil to cover the pork to 400°F (205°C). It may splatter so have a shield or lid ready. Carefully lower the pork into the oil, skin-side down. Fry for 12 to 15 minutes, until golden brown and crispy.

Remove the pork to a rack to allow airflow all around until it cool to the touch. Slice the pork into long strips, following the score lines. Your pork belly is now ready to eat or use for multiple dishes like Stir-Fried Chinese Broccoli with Crispy Pork Belly (Khana Moo Krob; page 74), basil pork belly, a pork belly BBQ plate and more.

NORTHERN THAI SAUSAGE (Sai Ua)

Northern Thai sausage is spicy and herbaceous and typically served with sticky rice, chilies, garlic and fresh cold veggies. You can also make this without a meat grinder by buying pre-ground pork and grinding your spices and herbs in a food processor. However, it's tough to make without a sausage stuffer.

MAKES: 6-8 SERVINGS

Supplies
Meat grinder

Sausage stuffer

Sausage pricker or equivalent

Ingredients
2 lb (907 g) skinless, boneless pork shoulder

3 tsp (15 g) kosher salt

1 tbsp (8 g) chopped galanga

2 tbsp (7 g) chopped cilantro stems

2 tbsp (30 ml) fish sauce

5 shallots, peeled & sliced

2 stalks lemongrass, tough outer leaves discarded, thinly sliced

10 kaffir lime leaves, cut into ribbons

10 cloves garlic, smashed

10 dried Thai chilies

1½ tbsp (18 g) turmeric powder

Sausage casing, 32–35 mm, pre-hanked recommended (see Pro Tip)

Freeze all the meat grinder parts for at least several hours or overnight.

Trim and discard any glands or discolored bits on the pork, then cut the pork into ¾-inch (2-cm) dice. Place the pork cubes in the freezer to get very cold, but not frozen solid, about 40 minutes. Meanwhile, you can use this time to chop and measure the remaining ingredients.

When you're ready to start the sausage, first, set up the grinder with the largest die size, according to the manufacturer's directions. Pass all the seasonings and aromatics through the grinder, using a few pieces of meat if needed to push them through. These will go through the grinder another time, so they don't need to be perfect. Mix these seasonings with the cold pork cubes.

Next, begin grinding the meat and seasonings. Because everything is nice and cold, you will get a nice grind with the fat cut rather than smeared. The mix should look like pink meat pieces and white fat pieces with flecks of chili and seasonings, and should not be a uniform pink color. After the last meat cubes have been fed into the grinder, you can put in a few small ice cubes to help push the last cubes of meat through the worm and the blade. Stop the grinder when the ice starts to come out of the die.

Mix the loose sausage by hand just to distribute the seasonings. Be careful not to knead it like bread, because too much handling can make the sausage tough. The sausage at this point should have a golden color from the turmeric, be evenly homogenous and have a sticky texture. Press plastic film directly onto the surface of the sausage to protect it from getting dry and place it in the refrigerator to get cold again. This can be for 1 to 2 hours or even overnight.

(continued)

NORTHERN THAI SAUSAGE (Sai Ua) (continued)

Prepare the stuffer to form the sausage. Rinse the casing by running water over both the outside and inside. Rub a little oil on the funnel of the stuffer and load the casing on it. This recipe will make about 40 inches (1 m) of sausage at the 32–35 mm size, so you don't need a long continuous casing. Lightly prick holes in the casing on the stuffer tube. Tie the end of the casing.

Load the sausage into the stuffer and begin pushing it to form the sausage. The sausage should be plump but not in danger of bursting. If you happen to have a blowout, just tie off both sides and continue until all the sausage has been formed into the casing. Lightly prick holes in the casing again to allow any air to escape. If you wish, you can make sausage links of your preferred size. At this point, the sausages can be cooked, but it's preferable to refrigerate again overnight to let the flavors marry.

Traditionally, this sausage is grilled over coals, but grilling from a raw state often means the fat leaks out and the result is a drier sausage. I prefer to precook the sausage in a 300°F (150°C) oven for about 15 minutes, or until it reaches an internal temperature of 150°F (65°C). From there, it can be grilled over a slow fire to get a little color, make the casing a little snappy and cook to a final internal temperature of 165°F (75°C).

Pro Tip: Sausage casing can be bought in many sizes and forms, but I recommend getting it already stretched onto a piece of plastic. Otherwise, it can be time consuming and frustrating to deal with untangling yards and yards of tiny membrane.

SEAFOOD

OCEAN & RIVER TREASURES

Thailand has an abundant seafood cookery history due to its geography. With the Andaman Sea to the south and the vast river systems, almost every single region of the country enjoys seafood. And before you write in and @ me, Britannica defines seafood as edible aquatic animals, excluding mammals, but including both freshwater and ocean creatures. With such a variety of ample seafood, Thai people have created ways to enjoy the abundance in traditional and non-traditional ways. From steamed mussels (page 133) to crispy fish floss covered with sweet and spicy mangoes (page 127), Thai seafood deserves its own cookbook, and maybe I'll write it one day. For now, enjoy some of my favorite recipes.

THAI SHRIMP CAKES (Tod Mun Goong)

These shrimp cakes are popular crispy nuggets you find on the streets in Thailand. They are delicious and easy to eat while in transit or for a quick snack. This dish is also one of the few that's enjoyed with sriracha. This isn't a place to worry about using large, expensive shrimp. Because the shrimp are ground into a paste, any size will do, which also makes me believe this dish was created to further utilize shrimp.

MAKES: 4 SERVINGS

Canola or other high-temperature cooking oil

2 lb (907 g) medium shrimp, peeled and deveined

2 cloves garlic, peeled

1 tsp white sugar

1 egg

½ tsp kosher salt

½ tsp white pepper

½ cup (104 g) ground pork

2 tbsp (30 g) roasted rice powder (see Pro Tip on page 180)

2 cups (112 g) panko breadcrumbs

Thai sriracha, plum sauce or sweet chili sauce, for serving

Preheat about 3 inches (8 cm) of cooking oil to between 350°F and 375°F (175°C and 190°C) in a 4- to 6-quart (3.8- to 5.7-L) Dutch oven or deep skillet.

While the oil is heating, place the shrimp and garlic in a large food processor and pulse intermittently into an even paste, about 1 minute. Add the sugar, egg, salt, pepper, pork and roasted rice powder. Process until thoroughly combined, about 10 seconds. Remove the shrimp mixture from the food processor and place in a medium bowl.

Place the panko breadcrumbs in a separate medium bowl.

With lightly oiled hands, take 2 to 3 tablespoons (30 to 45 g) of the shrimp mixture and form it into a ball. Place the ball into the bowl of panko and press it into the panko until it becomes flat and well coated on the bottom. Turn it over and press the other side into the panko, making sure to coat both sides thoroughly. Tap off any excess panko and prepare to fry.

Fry in small batches for about 2 minutes on each side, until golden brown and cooked through. Transfer the cooked shrimp cakes to a wire rack to drain. The cooked shrimp cakes can be kept warm in a 250°F (120°C) oven until they are all finished frying and you are ready to serve.

I like to serve these shrimp cakes with plum sauce, Thai sriracha or sweet chili sauce.

CLAMS IN ROASTED CHILI SAUCE (Hoy Lai Pad Prik Pao)

Southern Thailand is surrounded by water with the Gulf of Thailand and the Andaman Sea on either side. Phenomenal fishing, diving and ocean sports are everywhere. There's great shellfish, finfish and other seafood. This is my favorite way to eat clams, because the sweet, spicy and sticky sauce gets stuck in the open clams. Smash some jasmine rice into the clams—the rice grabs the sauce and makes a delicious bite.

MAKES: 4 SERVINGS

2 lb (907 g) fresh clams

2 tbsp (30 ml) canola or other high-temperature cooking oil

4 cloves garlic, minced

4 red Fresno or jalapeño chilies, thinly sliced

2 fresh Thai chilies, finely sliced

¼ cup (60 ml) Thai chili paste in soybean oil

2 tbsp (30 ml) oyster sauce

2 tsp (10 ml) Thai soybean sauce

2 tsp (10 ml) fish sauce

2 tsp (10 g) white sugar

2 cups (48 g) Thai sweet basil, stems removed and leaves torn

Pinch white pepper

Rinse the clams twice in clean water and scrub well. Remove any sand and make sure they are closed and alive. Discard any clams with cracked shells.

Warm a 9- to 11-inch (23- to 28-cm) skillet over high heat. Swirl in the oil. When you see wisps of white smoke, add the garlic, chilies and clams. Sauté until the garlic starts to brown, about 1 minute. Add the chili paste in soybean oil, oyster sauce, Thai soybean sauce, fish sauce and sugar and stir until well combined. Cover and continue cooking for about 1 minute, until the clams start to open. The sauce will get sticky and coat the clams.

Remove the lid, reduce the heat to low and stir in the basil leaves and white pepper. Give the mixture a few tosses to incorporate the basil. Taste and adjust the seasoning to your preference. Serve hot and make sure to discard any unopened clams.

CRISPY CATFISH RAFT SALAD WITH GREEN MANGO (Yum Pla Duk Foo)

I like to call this dish a catfish raft because of the airy and crispy puck of catfish that's suspended over the spicy, sour and sweet mango sauce. It took me years to figure out how to make this, and it is one of my favorite ways to prepare fish because it looks nothing like seafood. You can substitute the catfish with any flaky white meat fish like tilapia, halibut or even mahi-mahi.

MAKES: 2 SERVINGS

Yum Dressing

¼ cup (60 ml) fish sauce

¼ cup (60 ml) fresh lime juice

¼ cup (55 g) palm sugar or brown sugar

1 clove garlic, finely minced

1–2 fresh Thai chilies, minced

Salad

½ sour mango (about 4 oz [113 g]), julienned

½ cup (60 g) Chinese celery or regular celery leaves, cut into 2-inch (5-cm) pieces

1 cup (110 g) green apples, julienned

½ cup (4 g) cilantro leaves

½ cup (55 g) roasted cashews or peanuts, roughly chopped

Catfish

1 lb (454 g) catfish fillet

2 tsp (10 g) kosher salt

Canola or other high-temperature cooking oil, for frying

First, mix the ingredients for the yum dressing in a small bowl. Taste, and adjust any of the amounts if you'd like.

For the salad, wash and prepare the mango, celery, green apple and cilantro, and place them in a large bowl. Pour the dressing over the mango mixture and toss well to coat with the dressing. Set aside to macerate.

Season the fish with the salt and place it in a microwave-safe dish. Cover the dish with plastic wrap and microwave on high for 6 minutes. This will steam the fish. Remove the dish from the microwave and transfer the cooked fish to a clean kitchen towel, leaving the liquid in the dish. Twist the towel in opposite directions to wring out all the moisture so the fish is dry. Transfer the fish to a mortar and pound it to separate the muscle fibers. It should look like dry, fluffy threads and small bits of fish.

Add enough oil to fill one quarter of a high-sided pot. Preheat the oil to 375°F (190°C). The bubbling oil will expand significantly, so be sure to only fill the pot about a quarter full, leaving several inches of room. Set out a sheet pan with a wire rack or paper towels.

(continued)

CRISPY CATFISH RAFT SALAD WITH GREEN MANGO (Yum Pla Duk Foo) (continued)

Divide the fish into three portions. Put the first third into a spider or a small bowl. When the oil has reached temperature, take a pot lid in one hand as a shield and use the other hand to carefully scatter the fish evenly across the hot oil. If the oil threatens to overflow the pot, pause on adding more fish until the bubbles subside a bit.

With a slotted spoon or spider, gently loosen the raft from the sides of the pan so it can float freely. When it is a light golden brown, flip the raft over to crisp the bottom. When it is golden brown on both sides, remove it with the slotted spoon or spider, drain well over the pot, then transfer to the wire rack or paper towels.

Let the oil come up to temperature again and repeat with the remaining fish. Serve immediately over the mango salad and garnished with the cashews.

DEEP-FRIED TROUT WITH GREEN MANGO SLAW (Pla Taud Mamuang Yum)

I love fried fresh fish. It's crispy, moist and reminds me of being on the Mekong River in Thailand. I've adapted this dish for an easy-to-find market fish. Trout is great fried because it's not too dense and has all the crispy bits I love—from the skin to the eyeballs. If you like a tamer fried fillet, that's fine, too. The juxtaposition of the dry, savory, crispy fish paired with the refreshing sweet-and-sour salad is delicious. I made this dish during my *Iron Chef* battle with Morimoto and nearly beat him with it.

MAKES: 4 SERVINGS

2 lb (907 g) trout fillets, scaled

Kosher salt

Ground black pepper

2 shallots, finely sliced

1 clove garlic, finely chopped

1–3 fresh Thai chilies, sliced thin

½ cup (120 ml) fish sauce

½ cup (110 g) palm sugar or brown sugar

½ cup (120 ml) fresh lime juice

1½ qt (1.4 L) canola or other high-temperature cooking oil, for frying

3 eggs

2 cups (250 g) cornstarch

2 cups (112 g) panko breadcrumbs

2 cups (280 g) matchstick-cut green mango (flesh from 2 mangoes, or green apples are a great sub)

½ red onion, thinly sliced

½ cup (55 g) roasted salted cashews

¼ cup (4 g) cilantro leaves

Cut the trout filets in half, remove any bones and season lightly with salt and pepper. Thoroughly pat them dry with paper towels and set aside.

In a small saucepan, combine the shallots, garlic and Thai chilies over low heat. Stir in the fish sauce and sugar. Let the mixture heat up to just below a simmer. Stir it until the sugar dissolves, then remove it from the heat and add the lime juice. Transfer the mixture to a bowl and chill it in the refrigerator until ready to assemble the salad.

Heat the oil in a 4- to 5-quart (3.8- to 4.7-L) Dutch oven or pot until the oil reaches 360°F (180°C).

In a medium bowl, crack the eggs and whisk until evenly mixed. To another bowl, add the cornstarch. Place the panko breadcrumbs in a third bowl. Congrats, you've just created a breading station! First, dredge the fish in cornstarch and shake off the excess. Next, dip the fish in the eggs, then immediately roll it in panko. Knock off any excess panko and gently place the fish into the fryer, working in batches if needed. Fry the fish for about 5 minutes on each side, until cooked through and golden brown and delicious. Drain it on paper towels.

When you're ready to serve the fish, remove the dressing from the fridge and add the mango, red onion, cashews and cilantro, tossing to combine. Taste and adjust any of the flavors in the slaw if you'd like. Place the slaw over the fish and serve immediately.

FRIED TILAPIA WITH THREE-FLAVOR SAUCE

(Pla Tub Tim Thod Sam Rod)

Crispy fried fish bathed in a spicy and sweet sauce is fundamentally Thai. You'll find this dish along the banks of the extensive river systems that run through Thailand. It's also common to see this application on saltwater fish in the south, but that's the beauty of Thailand and the diversity of our food. You can substitute any of your favorite whole fried fish and bump up the spice by subbing Thai chilies for the Fresno peppers.

MAKES: 2 SERVINGS

Fish

1 large whole tilapia (about 2 lb [907 g]), scaled and gutted

Kosher salt

Ground black pepper

Canola or other high-temperature cooking oil, for deep-frying

1 cup (128 g) cornstarch

Sauce

2 tbsp (30 ml) canola or other high-temperature cooking oil

3 cloves garlic, roughly chopped

2 long red Fresno chilies, stems removed and small diced

1 red or green bell pepper, medium diced

¼ cup (60 ml) tamarind concentrate

¼ cup (55 g) palm sugar or brown sugar

2 tbsp (30 ml) fish sauce

2 tbsp (30 ml) fresh lime juice

1 tbsp (8 g) cornstarch mixed with 1 tbsp (15 ml) water to make a slurry

2 scallions, thinly sliced on the bias, for garnish

To make the fish, pat the fish dry inside and out with paper towels. Score each side two to three times down to the bone to allow the oil to penetrate. Season both sides generously with salt and pepper. Heat about 4 inches (10 cm) of oil in a 4- to 5-quart (3.8- to 4.7-L) Dutch oven or pot until the oil reaches 360°F (180°C). Prepare a sheet pan with a wire rack or a large plate with paper towels.

Place the cornstarch in a bowl wide enough to hold the fish. Dredge the fish in the cornstarch on both sides until it is well coated. Knock off any excess and carefully place the fish into the hot oil. Fry the fish for 3 to 5 minutes on each side, until cooked through. Transfer the cooked fish to the rack or drain over paper towels.

While the fish is frying, make the sauce. Heat a wok or large skillet over high heat and add the 2 tablespoons (30 ml) of oil. When a wisp of white smoke appears, add the garlic, chilies and bell pepper and cook for about 1 minute, until the peppers start to soften. Stir in the tamarind concentrate, sugar, fish sauce and lime juice and cook until the sugar dissolves and the sauce comes together, about 1 minute. When the sauce reaches a boil, stir in the cornstarch slurry. Constantly stir until the sauce thickens, then turn off the heat.

Place the fish on a plate, then smother with the three-flavor sauce and garnish with the scallions.

> **Pro Tip:** This recipe also works great with fish fillets such as halibut, salmon or cod.

STEAMED MUSSELS WITH THAI HERBS IN SPICY BROTH

(Hoy Malaengphoo Nung)

This is my version of a dish that originated at Jitlada in Los Angeles. The current family that runs Jitlada is from southern Thailand, but this dish predates even the Singsanong family back to the original owners. I like using frozen New Zealand mussels because they are flash-frozen, which means they're always fresh, plus they're already cleaned and super sweet. That said, I would also use this recipe on any freshly harvested mussel.

MAKES: 4 SERVINGS

2 lb (907 g) live mussels or frozen New Zealand mussels (not defrosted)

2 tbsp (30 ml) canola or other high-temperature cooking oil

2 cloves garlic, chopped

1 shallot

1 stalk lemongrass, tough outer leaves discarded and thinly sliced on the bias

3 kaffir lime leaves

4 thin slices galanga

2–3 whole Thai or dried chilies, smashed to expose the seeds

1 tbsp (15 g) chili paste in soybean oil

2½ cups (590 ml) Thai Chicken Stock (page 41) or plain chicken stock

½ cup (12 g) Thai sweet basil leaves

½ cup (8 g) roughly chopped cilantro

2 tbsp (30 ml) fish sauce

2 tbsp (30 ml) fresh lime juice

If using fresh mussels, rinse the mussels and scrub well. Remove any barnacles and beards and make sure they are closed and alive. Discard any mussels with cracked shells.

Heat a 4-quart (3.8-L) lidded saucepan over high heat for about 30 seconds. Swirl in the oil and heat until you see wisps of white smoke. Add the garlic, shallot, lemongrass, kaffir lime leaves, galanga and dried chilies to the pot. Sauté for 1 to 2 minutes until fragrant and heated through.

Add the chili paste in soybean oil and chicken stock to the pot, and give it a good stir to dissolve the paste. Add the mussels to the pot and cover. Let the broth come to a boil and cook the mussels until they open, 2 to 3 minutes. If using frozen New Zealand mussels, they will not open but will be cooked through.

Remove the lid and add the basil and cilantro. Stir them into the broth and let cook for about 30 seconds. Turn off the heat and stir in the fish sauce and lime juice. Taste and adjust the seasonings if you'd like. If you used fresh mussels, discard any that did not open. Pieces of galanga and lemongrass are generally not eaten so either fish them out or warn your guests not to eat them. Serve hot.

APPS & SMALL PLATES TO SHARE

Thais are notorious grazers and don't often eat one long multicourse meal. We want deliciousness but usually don't want it to take forever. I've collected these appetizers and small plates very purposefully. Any recipe in this section is great as a delicious snack on its own, or can be combined with other recipes in this section for a family-style meal or made into a portable to-go meal.

THAI CRISPY SPRING ROLLS (Popia Taud)

The difference between egg rolls and spring rolls are the feeling but also the wrappers. Egg roll wrappers are doughier and fry up with little holes in them. Spring roll wrappers fry up tight, airy and very crispy. They eat a lot lighter than egg rolls. These Thai spring rolls are similar to Vietnamese egg rolls.

MAKES: 12 ROLLS

6 oz (170 g) coarse-ground pork

1 cup (2 oz [55 g]) dried glass noodles, soaked in warm water

3 medium dried shiitake mushrooms, soaked in warm water

1 shallot, minced

½ cup (20 g) shredded carrot

1 scallion, thinly sliced

1 clove garlic, finely minced

1 tbsp (15 g) white sugar

2 tbsp (30 ml) fish sauce

1 tsp kosher salt

Heavy pinch ground black pepper

Canola or other high-temperature cooking oil, for frying

12 medium-sized (8.5-inch [22-cm] square) pastry wrappers

1 egg, beaten slightly, to help seal the rolls

Thai sweet chili sauce, for dipping

To make the filling, add the ground pork to a mixing bowl. Drain the soaked noodles and cut them into approximately 1-inch (3-cm) pieces. Drain the soaked mushrooms, remove the stems and cut the caps into a small dice. Add the noodles and mushrooms to the bowl with the pork, along with the shallot, carrot, scallion, garlic, sugar, fish sauce, salt and black pepper. Mix well to incorporate everything evenly into the pork. Allow the mixture to rest for 15 minutes, or make this ahead and store it in the fridge until you're ready to cook.

In a 6- to 8-quart (5.7- to 7.6-L) Dutch oven, preheat about 5 inches (13 cm) of the oil to 360°F (180°C).

While the oil is heating, peel off a sheet of pastry wrapper and place it on a work surface with one of the points facing down (in a diamond orientation). Scoop out a Ping Pong ball–sized portion of the pork filling, about 1½ ounces (43 g). Place the filling in the center of the pastry. Take the southern corner and bring it up to the northern corner. Applying gentle pressure with your fingers, pull back to shape and tuck the filling into a cylinder about 3 inches (8 cm) in length. Flatten the sides of the tube and fold inward. Use a pastry brush to brush a little of the beaten egg near the northern corner and roll the package forward to complete the roll. Place it seam-side down and form the remaining rolls.

When the oil has reached temperature, carefully fry the rolls in two batches (or more if necessary) until the wrappers are golden brown and crispy, and the filling has reached 165°F (75°C) internal temperature. Remove the rolls to a rack or a tray lined with paper towels to drain excess oil. Serve with Thai sweet chili sauce.

Pro Tips: You can freeze these spring rolls before frying. Also if you have leftover fried rolls, one of my favorite ways to reheat them is in the air fryer set to 375°F (190°C), full fan.

GRILLED PORK STICKS (Moo Ping)

Literally translated to "grilled pork," moo ping is a street food specialty of sticky, garlic-marinated pork on skewers. Almost always paired with sticky rice, it's one of the most perfect foods. Pork butt has the perfect balance of flavor and texture in my opinion, but you can substitute pork loin or tenderloin in this recipe.

MAKES: 10–12 SKEWERS

3 cloves garlic, minced

1 tsp white pepper

1½ tbsp (5 g) cilantro roots (stems are okay if you can't find roots)

¼ cup (60 ml) Thai soybean sauce

2 tbsp (30 ml) sweet soy sauce

2 tbsp (28 g) palm sugar or brown sugar

3 tbsp (45 ml) fish sauce

3 tbsp (45 ml) oyster sauce

2 lb (907 g) pork butt

10-15 (6-inch [15-cm]) bamboo skewers, soaked

Oil or cooking spray, for grilling

To make the marinade, combine the garlic, pepper, cilantro, soybean sauce, sweet soy sauce, sugar, fish sauce and oyster sauce in a mini food processor. Pulse four to six times, until all the ingredients blend into a smooth marinade.

Slice the pork against the grain into 1½-inch (4-cm) square tiles about ¼ inch (6 mm) thick. Combine the pork and the marinade in a large bowl, and massage the pork to coat it evenly. Cover and let marinate for 4 hours or overnight.

Thread the pork onto the bamboo skewers, leaving 2 inches (5 cm) at the bottom of each skewer. You can cook them immediately or freeze the pork sticks, wrapped tightly, for up to 2 months.

When ready to cook, heat a grill or grill pan to high and preheat it for at least 5 minutes. Rub a little oil on the grill or spray with pan spray. Grill the pork for 3 to 5 minutes on the first side, until you get a nice brown color. Flip and cook for another 3 to 5 minutes, until just cooked through.

Pro Tip: You can substitute boneless chicken thighs or your favorite steak cuts in this recipe. I make these in big batches and freeze them raw on the stick tightly wrapped. You can defrost them in the fridge the day before you cook them, and it actually makes them more tender.

FRIED WONTONS (Keow Taud)

Wonton soup is not the only way to enjoy these delicious dumplings. As a kid, I loved starting my meal with fried crispy wontons served with sweet chili sauce. You can use this recipe to make poached wontons for soup as well.

MAKES: 24 WONTONS

1 lb (454 g) coarsely ground lean pork

1 lb (454 g) medium shrimp, peeled, deveined and coarsely chopped

2 tbsp (30 ml) thin soy sauce

2 tbsp (30 ml) oyster sauce

Few drops sesame oil

2 tsp (10 ml) sherry

1 tsp white sugar

1 scallion, minced

1 tsp cornstarch

Pinch salt

Pinch white pepper

24 wonton wrappers

1 egg, lightly beaten, for sealing

2 qt (1.9 L) canola or other high-temperature cooking oil

Sweet chili sauce or plum sauce, for serving

Combine the pork, shrimp, soy sauce, oyster sauce, sesame oil, sherry, sugar, scallion, cornstarch, salt and pepper in a large bowl, mixing them together well. Lay one wonton wrapper in front of you. Moisten all the edges of the wonton wrapper with the beaten egg. Place a heaping teaspoon of filling in the center, then fold over to make a triangle. With both hands hold the triangle by the two widest corners then push down so that the filled center folds up similar to a tortellini.

Place the completed wontons on a tray. Uncooked, the wontons can be wrapped and kept frozen for 1 to 2 weeks then dropped into the fryer frozen.

When ready to cook, heat the oil in a 4- or 5-quart (3.8- or 4.7-L) Dutch oven or pot until the oil reaches 360°F (180°C). Working in small batches, fry the wontons until golden, about 2 minutes on each side. Drain on a wire rack placed over a cookie sheet.

I like to serve the wontons with sweet chili or plum sauce.

STUFFED CHICKEN WINGS

aka Angel Wings (Peek Gai Yat Sai)

We served this dish in our first Thai restaurant when I was a kid. I loved these stuffed chicken wings then and continue to make these for my kids. The technique removes most of the bones and turns a wing into a boneless drumstick. It might seem difficult at first, but you'll get the deboning technique after a few tries.

MAKES: 4 SERVINGS

6 whole large chicken wings (about 1¼ lb [567 g])

3 medium dried shiitake mushrooms

1 cup (2 oz [55 g]) dried glass noodles, soaked in warm water

6 oz (170 g) ground pork (ideally coarse ground)

1 shallot, minced

½ cup (20 g) shredded carrot

1 scallion, thinly sliced

1 clove garlic, finely minced

1 tbsp (15 g) white sugar

2 tbsp (30 ml) fish sauce

1 tsp kosher salt

Heavy pinch ground black pepper

Canola or other high-temperature cooking oil, for frying

1 cup (128 g) cornstarch or potato starch

3 eggs

3 cups (168 g) panko breadcrumbs

Thai sriracha

Sweet chili sauce or plum sauce

Sliced cucumbers and carrots

To prep the chicken wings, begin by removing the large drumette bone by carving the skin and connective tissue around the top of the bone. Pull the skin and meat back from the bone until you reach the end of the bone. Separate the bone from the wing. Next, remove the two bones from the middle section by cutting the cartilage cap, exposing the bones. When the meat and skin are separated from the bones, pull it down like a sleeve until you reach the joint connected to the wing tip. Using a dry paper towel for grip, rotate each one until it pops out. Now you have a wing tip and a boneless section that will act as a pocket for the stuffing. Place them in the fridge until you're ready to stuff.

To make the stuffing, soak the mushrooms in a small bowl with hot water (enough to cover them) for about 15 minutes. Meanwhile, drain the glass noodles and use scissors to cut the glass noodles into 1-inch (3-cm) pieces. Place the glass noodles in a large bowl. Add the ground pork, shallot, carrot, scallion, garlic, sugar, fish sauce, salt and pepper.

By now the mushrooms should be reconstituted; drain them, give them a good squeeze to remove as much liquid as possible and mince them finely. Add the mushrooms to the filling mix in the bowl. I like using my hands to mix, but feel free to glove up if you prefer. Massage the mixture together until fully combined and there are no clumps of any single ingredient, 1 to 2 minutes.

When you're ready to stuff, make sure the wings are very dry. Pat them down with paper towels to make sure you don't have any excess moisture inside. This can lead to bubbles and blowouts when frying. Scoop out about ½ cup (100 g) of filling and start filling the wing at the opening where the two bones were. Fill tightly; each wing should be able to take about ½ to ¾ cup (100 to 150 g) of filling. Clean off any excess filling sticking out the top and repeat until all the wings are stuffed.

(continued)

STUFFED CHICKEN WINGS

aka Angel Wings (Peek Gai Yat Sai) (continued)

Fill a 4- to 6-quart (3.8- to 5.7-L) Dutch oven with 3 inches (8 cm) of oil and heat to 365°F (185°C). Make a fry station by setting out three medium-sized bowls. Add the cornstarch to the first bowl. Crack the eggs into the second bowl and whisk well. Add the panko to the third bowl. When the oil reaches temperature, start by dredging a stuffed wing with cornstarch, coating evenly on all sides. Knock off any excess cornstarch, then coat with the eggs from the second bowl. Immediately go from the egg right into the panko breadcrumbs. Press both sides gently into the panko, knock off the excess, then place the coated wing right into the fryer. Fry in small batches, making sure the oil never drops below 350°F (175°C). Fry each wing for 3 to 4 minutes on each side until golden brown and cooked through (the internal temperature should reach 165°F [75°C]).

You can slice each wing into thirds or serve whole. I love serving these wings with Thai sriracha, sweet chili sauce or plum sauce and some crisp cold veggies like cucumbers and carrots.

ROTI BREAD

Thai Buddhism and many spices and dishes are a direct influence from Indian culture. These are basically Indian paratha bread made from wheat flour, then oiled and layered to be cooked on a hot flattop. The most common way to eat them is a sweet version by adding sugar and condensed milk. I also like to pair them with curry as a starch and an eating implement. Break off a chunk of bread, dunk it into curry and grab a piece of chicken on the way out.

MAKES: 8 FLATBREADS

½ cup (120 ml) water

1 tbsp (15 g) white sugar

½ tsp kosher salt

¼ cup (60 ml) milk

1 egg

4 tbsp (56 g) unsalted butter, melted

3 cups (375 g) all-purpose flour

Cooking oil

To the bowl of a stand mixer, add the water, sugar and salt. Stir well to dissolve the sugar and salt. Add the milk, egg and melted butter. Using a fork, scramble the egg for about 10 seconds and mix the ingredients together. Add the flour to the bowl, then attach the dough hook to the mixer, and knead on low for about 7 minutes. The dough should be tacky but not sticking to the container or your hand. This dough is quite wet compared to regular bread dough. Stretching the dough between your fingers should make a small windowpane.

Prepare a separate resting container for the dough by oiling the inside of the container and adding some oil to the bottom of the container. Oil your hands.

Divide the dough into eight equal pieces, each about the size of a golf ball or slightly larger. Form each ball by pulling a side of the ball and tucking it in the middle. Rotate and repeat the pulling and tucking until the ball is smooth. It should not take more than half a minute per ball. Finally, push the dough from the bottom through the space between your thumb and your index finger. The ball should be smooth and tight. Tuck the rest in and pinch it together.

Oil the dough ball and place it in the oiled container. Form the rest of the dough balls and let them sit and bathe in the oil for at least 20 minutes. You can also leave them out overnight. Do not refrigerate. The resting period is very important as it lets the gluten relax. The relaxed dough is easier to spread out during slapping.

(continued)

ROTI BREAD (continued)

Place a dough ball on an oiled work surface. Flatten the ball, then use a small rolling pin or your flat palm to spread it into a circle about ¼ inch (6 mm) thick. Sprinkle with a few drops of oil. Using a knife or dough scraper, make a cut to the middle of the circle. Start with the cut and roll the dough around until you meet the end of the cut, forming a tight cone. Then take the thick side with a lot of layers and start opening up the layers and flattening into a disc. This will create a layering effect. Roll the disc ¼ inch (6 mm) thick. Repeat until all the dough balls are cut, rolled and layered.

Heat a heavy skillet, preferably cast iron, over medium-high heat for about 3 minutes, until hot. Place one roti on the hot skillet. Cook until golden brown on the bottom, then flip and repeat cooking the other side, for about 5 minutes total. Repeat until all the rotis are cooked.

ISAAN CHICKEN LAARB (Laap Gai Isaan)

This tangier version of chicken laarb salad is influenced by the Isaan, or northeastern, area of Thailand. By contrast, the northern version is more savory than the Isaan version, with a variety of pork offal meats like liver and cracklins. Northern food is very healthy and delicious. Always serve this dish with a variety of fresh raw vegetables.

MAKES: 4–6 SERVINGS

1 tbsp (15 ml) tamarind concentrate

1½ lb (680 g) ground chicken breast

1 tbsp (15 ml) canola or other high-temperature cooking oil

3 cloves garlic, minced

1 large shallot, thinly sliced

¼ cup (60 ml) fish sauce

½ cup (120 ml) fresh lime juice

½ cup (110 g) palm sugar or brown sugar

1–2 tsp (3–6 g) Thai chili powder

½ cup (46 g) mint leaves

½ red onion, thinly sliced

¼ cup (55 g) roasted rice powder (see Pro Tip on page 180)

3–4 scallions, thinly sliced on the bias

Thin-sliced red onion

Thin-sliced cucumber

Green cabbage wedges

Stir the tamarind concentrate into the ground chicken in a large bowl and let it stand for 15 minutes.

Heat a medium-sized pan over high heat and add the oil. When you see the first wisps of white smoke appear, sauté the garlic and shallot until the shallot becomes translucent, about 1 minute. Fold in the chicken and stir-fry until the chicken is just cooked through, 3 to 4 minutes. If any liquid is released, either drain it or reduce it so it does not dilute the seasonings.

Turn off the heat, then stir in the fish sauce, lime juice, sugar and chili powder and mix well. Adjust the flavors as necessary to your taste. Fold in the mint, red onion, roasted rice powder and scallions (reserving some scallions for garnish) until well combined. Garnish with the reserved scallions and serve with the red onion, sliced cucumber and cabbage wedges.

CHICKEN SATAY (Satay Gai)

The original Thai fusion dish, satay comes from Indonesia and Malaysia. But the Thai version, in my humble opinion, has a better range of flavors. The meat is more savory and the sauce is sweeter, but in a pleasant way. It draws on the influence of Indians, Muslims and Arabs traveling through Thailand trading spices and textiles.

My tip for this dish is using Thai curry paste for its incredible amount of herbs, which will bring a lot of flavor to the meat. This recipe uses chicken but any of your favorite proteins will make a delicious satay.

MAKES: 10–12 SKEWERS

2 tsp (14 g) red curry paste

1 tbsp (6 g) curry powder

½ tbsp (8 g) ground black pepper

1 tbsp (15 g) kosher salt

1 tbsp (15 g) white sugar

1 tsp garlic powder, or more to taste

¼ cup (60 ml) full-fat coconut milk

2 lb (907 g) chicken breast

10–15 (6-inch [15-cm]) bamboo skewers, soaked

Oil or cooking spray, for grilling

Thai Peanut Sauce (page 204), for serving

To make the marinade, combine the curry paste, curry powder, pepper, salt, sugar, garlic powder and coconut milk in a medium bowl.

Slice the chicken against the grain into 2-inch (5-cm) square tiles about ¼ inch (6 mm) thick. Add the chicken to the marinade and massage it with your hands to coat it evenly. Thread the chicken onto the bamboo skewers, leaving 2 inches (5 cm) at the bottom of each skewer. You can cook the skewers immediately or cover and marinate in the fridge overnight for better flavor and tenderness.

Heat a grill or griddle to high and preheat for at least 5 minutes. Rub a little oil on the grill or spray with pan spray. Cook the chicken for 3 to 5 minutes on the first side or until you get a nice brown color. Flip and cook for another 3 to 5 minutes until just cooked through. Serve with the peanut sauce.

THAI-STYLE STEAMED DUMPLINGS (Kanom Jeeb)

These are the Thai version of Chinese shumai dumplings. There's a lot of Chinese influence in Thai foods like noodles and rice. My grandparents immigrated from China to Thailand, as did so many others, and this is a comfort food from southern China to many Thai-Chinese.

MAKES: 24 DUMPLINGS

10 dried Chinese black mushrooms

1½ lb (680 g) coarsely ground pork

1 lb (450 g) shrimp, peeled, deveined and coarsely chopped

1 tsp kosher salt

4 tsp (20 g) white sugar

1 tbsp (15 ml) peanut oil

¼ cup (60 ml) oyster sauce

2 tbsp (30 ml) fish sauce

2 tsp (6 g) cornstarch

2 tbsp (30 ml) sesame oil

Pinch white pepper

24 Hong Kong–style round dumpling skins or wonton skins

2 large carrots, cut into ¼-inch (6-mm) squares

Grandma's Everything Dipping Sauce (page 205, optional)

Soak the mushrooms in hot water for 30 minutes to reconstitute them. Drain and rinse the mushrooms, remove the stems and chop them into a small dice.

In a large bowl, combine the soaked mushrooms, pork, shrimp, salt, sugar, peanut oil, oyster sauce, fish sauce, cornstarch, sesame oil and pepper and mix until well combined. You can also use a mixer with the paddle attachment for this. Cover the bowl and let it rest in the refrigerator for at least 1 hour or overnight.

When you're ready to cook, lay a dumpling skin on your work surface. Cover the remaining dumpling skins with a damp towel to keep them from drying out. Place about 2 tablespoons (30 g) of filling in the center. Hold the filling in place with your fingers and use the other hand to twist the skin around the filling. While twisting, place three carrot pieces in the top center. Make sure to flatten the top of the filling into the skin. Place the bottom of the dumpling on the work surface and flatten it out. Repeat this process until all the filling is gone.

Set up a bamboo steamer over a pot with at least 4 inches (10 cm) of boiling water. Steam the dumplings in a steamer basket over high heat for about 7 minutes, or until cooked through. Serve hot, either plain or with dipping sauce. My favorite sauce with these is Grandma's Everything Dipping Sauce (page 205).

THAI SAVORY BITES (Miang Kham)

This royal one-bite dish is usually eaten during the rainy season when the betel leaves (cheu pru) are plentiful. Kings have written about this dish and its beauty. If you can't find betel leaves, substitute with large spinach leaves.

MAKES: 4 SERVINGS

Filling

1 cup (96 g) unsweetened grated coconut

½ cup (80 g) finely diced shallots

½ cup (112 g) finely diced whole lime (with peel)

¼ cup (24 g) peeled and finely diced fresh ginger

½ cup (19 g) finely diced dried shrimp

½ cup (60 g) unsalted roasted peanuts

3–5 fresh Thai chilies, finely diced

Sauce

1 tbsp (15 g) Thai shrimp paste

½ tbsp (4 g) chopped galanga

½ tbsp (5 g) chopped shallot

2 tbsp (8 g) unsweetened shredded coconut

3 tbsp (7 g) chopped dried shrimp

1 tsp grated ginger

2 tbsp (30 ml) canola or other high-temperature cooking oil

2 tbsp (30 ml) fish sauce

2 cups (440 g) palm sugar or brown sugar

1½ cups (360 ml) water

Assembly

20–30 la lot leaves (Vietnamese), aka cheu pru leaves (Thai)

Preheat the oven to 350°F (175°C) and line a sheet pan with parchment paper. Spread the coconut on the parchment-lined pan and place in the oven. Toast until brown, 12 to 15 minutes, rotating the pan every 5 minutes.

To make the sauce, add the shrimp paste, galanga, shallot, shredded coconut, dried shrimp and ginger to a spice grinder that has a removable top. Pulse the ingredients until a fine paste is formed. You can add 1 teaspoon (5 ml) of water if the ingredients aren't grinding.

Heat the oil in a medium skillet over high heat for about 1 minute. Add the paste to the skillet and fry until the paste is browned and fragrant, 1 to 2 minutes. Stir in the fish sauce, sugar and water to combine. Let the sauce come to a full boil and cook for about 10 minutes, until it reduces to a glaze that coats the back of a wooden spoon. Remove the sauce from the heat and reserve.

To serve, arrange each filling ingredient in a separate pile or in separate bowls. Make individual packages by filling one leaf with a little of each filling, then top with a little sauce. Guests should make them as they eat.

FRIED THAI FISH CAKES (Tod Mun Pla)

These are fish fritters that almost eat like sausage patties. This recipe is a great way to utilize any flaky-fleshed fish. The real key to these is the fried basil that gets mixed into the patties. Don't overmix the fish cakes as they can get too dense and become rubbery. You can bump up the spice by adding Thai chilies or a little more of the red curry paste.

MAKES: 8–10 FISH CAKES

Canola or other high-temperature cooking oil, for frying

1 cup (24 g) Thai basil leaves (leaves picked from the stems)

1½ lb (680 g) white fish fillets, such as barramundi, cod or halibut

2 eggs

2–3 tbsp (42–63 g) red curry paste

1 tsp fish sauce

2 tsp (10 g) white sugar

½ tsp kosher salt

½ tsp white pepper

¼ cup (25 g) Thai long beans or green beans, finely sliced

2 kaffir lime leaves, fine julienne sliced

Sweet chili sauce or Ajad Sauce, aka Cucumber Relish for Satay (page 207), for serving

Preheat about 4 inches (10 cm) of the oil in a 4-quart (3.8-L) pot to 365°F (185°C). When the oil reaches temperature, carefully lower the basil into the oil. The basil will sputter and pop while frying. Fry for about 1 minute, until crispy and dark, translucent green. Remove and drain the fried basil on paper towels, and reserve for the filling. Turn the heat off until you're ready to fry the fish cakes.

Cut the fish fillets into 2-inch (5-cm) pieces and place the pieces in a large food processor with the blade attachment. Add the eggs, curry paste, fish sauce, sugar, salt and white pepper. Pulse in quick 1- to 2-second increments just until a smooth paste forms, about 1 minute.

Tip the paste out into a large bowl and, using a silicone spatula, work the green beans, kaffir lime leaves and fried Thai basil into the paste. Stir for 1 to 2 minutes, just until the ingredients are evenly incorporated. This can also be done in a stand mixer with the paddle attachment if you're making a large batch.

When you're ready to cook, heat the oil back to 365°F (185°C). Oil your hands with cold oil or cooking spray and form the fish mixture into flat patties, about 2 to 3 ounces (57 to 85 g) each, for a total of eight to ten fish patties. Working in batches, fry the patties in the hot oil for about 2 minutes, until golden brown and fully cooked. Drain on a wire rack or paper towels.

Serve hot with the sweet chili sauce or cucumber relish.

SAVORY PORK JERKY (Moo Dat Diow)

While not technically "jerky" because it's not dehydrated, these sweet, savory nuggets are a great snack by themselves or eaten with Thai sticky rice as a meal. They also travel incredibly well because they are glazed with soy and sugar and fried. I pack them for long trips and for my kids' lunches.

MAKES: 4 SERVINGS

1 lb (454 g) pork shoulder

1 clove garlic, minced

1 tsp white pepper

2 tbsp (30 ml) fish sauce

1 tbsp (15 ml) Thai soybean sauce

2 tbsp (30 ml) sweet soy sauce

1 tbsp (14 g) palm sugar or brown sugar

4 cups (960 ml) canola or other high-temperature cooking oil, for frying

Cut the pork into thin strips about 3 inches (8 cm) long and ½ inch (13 mm) wide. It's okay to trim any silver skin away, but don't trim off too much fat.

Combine the garlic, pepper, fish sauce, soybean sauce, sweet soy sauce and sugar in a blender and blend into a fine puree or until you can't detect any garlic bits in the marinade.

Place the pork in a bowl, pour the marinade over the pork and massage it well until the pork is completely coated. Marinate the pork, covered, in the refrigerator for at least 4 hours, or overnight.

Line a sheet pan with paper towels or parchment paper. Shake off the excess marinade, lay the pork on the sheet pan and pat dry with paper towels. Many cooks like to take an extra step and at this point dry the pork in the fridge overnight, uncovered. That will create a dryer jerky. I like a moister jerky so I cook it immediately.

Heat the oil in a medium saucepan over high heat. Bring the temperature up to about 375°F (190°C), and fry the pork strips in small batches. Cook for about 4 to 6 minutes, until cooked through and the edges are slightly crisp. Remove the pork from the oil and drain on paper towels.

SALADS & UMAMI VEGGIES

With Thailand's Buddhist history and the overall Southeast Asian diet with vegetables making up the majority of ingredients, there are hundreds of vegetable dishes that showcase the variety in flavors and techniques. You also see a lot of Chinese wok influence when it comes to vegetable stir-fries. On the other end of the spectrum, Thai salads with cold crispy "yum" dressings are unique to the culture. Spicy, sweet and tangy dressings that bathe crisp herbs and vegetables with animal protein as a garnish are uniquely Thai.

COCONUT MANGO SALAD WITH SHRIMP (Yum Mamuang)

There are hundreds, if not thousands, of mango varieties in the world. In Thailand, there is a green mango that is tart and very crisp. Green mangoes are great for crunchy salads or cut up to serve with dips. Some Asian markets will have them, but if you can't find them, just use an under-ripe mango for this recipe. You could also julienne Granny Smith apples for half of the recipe for some tang and crunch.

MAKES: 4 SERVINGS

1 tbsp (15 ml) canola or other high-temperature cooking oil

½ lb (226 g) medium shrimp peeled and deveined, sliced in half lengthwise

2 shallots, thinly sliced

2 cloves garlic, finely chopped

1–2 fresh Thai chilies, thinly sliced

⅓ cup (80 ml) fresh lime juice

⅓ cup (80 ml) fish sauce

½ cup (110 g) palm sugar or brown sugar

3 cups (420 g) green mango, cut into matchsticks

1 cup (60 g) toasted coconut chips (see Pro Tip)

½ red onion, very thinly sliced

3 scallions, thinly sliced on the bias

¼ cup (28 g) roasted cashews

Heat a medium skillet over medium and add the oil. When you see a wisp of white smoke, add the shrimp and lightly sauté them for about 1 minute. Reduce the heat to low and add the shallots, garlic and Thai chilies. Cook for an additional minute, until the shrimp are just cooked through.

Turn off the heat. Stir in the lime juice, fish sauce and sugar. Stir well until the sugar is dissolved. Transfer the shrimp and dressing to a serving bowl and allow it to cool for a few minutes.

When ready to serve, add the mango, coconut and red onion to the serving bowl. Toss to combine, and garnish with the scallions and cashews.

Pro Tip: You can buy unsweetened toasted coconut chips anywhere now, and they are perfect for this recipe!

THAI BEEF SALAD (Yum Neua)

This recipe uses a great marinade that would work for any meat you like to slap on the grill, like steaks, pork chops or even lamb chops. It also uses a great Thai dressing that you can serve on way more than just lettuce. Try it on anything you would call a salad.

The dressing calls for lemongrass and kaffir lime leaves, and you can use frozen versions of both. It's always tough to buy just a few leaves or stalks for a recipe, so when you do, chop your leftovers finely and keep them in a resealable plastic bag in the freezer.

MAKES: 4 SERVINGS

Thai Grilled Beef Marinade

2 lb (907 g) beef flank steak

¼ cup (60 g) minced garlic

¼ cup (30 g) minced cilantro stems

1 tsp white pepper

2 tbsp (30 ml) fish sauce

3 tbsp (45 ml) thin soy sauce

2 tbsp (30 g) white sugar

Salad Dressing

2 tbsp (30 ml) peanut oil

3 cloves garlic, minced

1 stalk lemongrass, tough outer leaves discarded, minced

3 kaffir lime leaves, very thinly sliced

½ cup (120 ml) fresh lime juice

½ cup (120 ml) fish sauce

⅓ cup (73 g) palm sugar or brown sugar, packed

Salad

6 cups (170 g) mixed salad greens

½ red onion, thinly sliced

1 English cucumber, seeded and thinly sliced

½ cup (46 g) mint leaves

2 scallions, chopped

To make the marinade, place the flank steak in a medium-large zip-top bag or bowl. Add all the remaining ingredients to the beef. Massage all the ingredients into the beef for about 1 minute. Seal the bag or cover and place it in the fridge for at least 2 hours, or overnight.

To make the dressing, heat a small saucepan over low heat. Add the oil, garlic, lemongrass and kaffir lime leaves and sweat for 1 minute, or until the garlic just starts to turn light brown. Remove from the heat and stir in the lime juice, fish sauce and brown sugar until thoroughly combined. Set aside.

To assemble the salad, heat a grill to high, and grill the marinated beef to your desired doneness, then slice it against the grain into thin strips. Add the salad greens, red onion and cucumbers with most of the dressing to a large bowl. Leave a few spoonfuls of dressing for drizzling. Toss the salad gently to combine.

Place the sliced grilled beef on top of the salad and garnish it with the mint leaves and scallions. Drizzle the remaining dressing on top of the salad.

PAPAYA SALAD (Som Tum Thai)

Green papayas are readily available at Asian and Latin markets. They are the same long papayas eaten ripe, just picked green and young. If they are tough to find, you can sub in a julienned fruit or vegetable blend, including carrots, apples and cabbage—all work great for this recipe. Thai salted shrimp are little, orange, bay-sized shrimp that have been salted and dried. They add amazing umami and salty flavor to this and any dish.

MAKES: 4 SERVINGS

Dressing

¼ cup (60 ml) fish sauce

¼ cup (60 ml) fresh lime juice

3 tbsp (42 g) palm sugar or brown sugar

1 tbsp (15 g) chili paste in soybean oil

1 tbsp (12 g) msg

2 cloves garlic, minced

1–3 fresh Thai chilies, minced

Salad

8–10 cherry tomatoes, quartered, divided

1 cup (85 g) green beans or long beans, cut on the bias into 1½-inch (4-cm) lengths, divided

4 cups (640 g) young green papaya, grated

1 cup (120 g) chopped roasted peanuts, divided

To make the dressing, place the dressing ingredients, four of the cherry tomatoes and ¼ cup (21 g) of the beans into a blender and pulse them together for about 5 seconds. The dressing should be slightly chunky, not smooth. Adjust the number of chilies depending on how spicy you like your food.

To assemble the salad, in a large bowl, toss the papaya, remaining tomatoes, remaining beans and some of the peanuts together with the dressing to taste. Make sure to aggressively mix the ingredients to slightly break up the tomatoes and beans. Garnish the salad with the remaining peanuts.

CRISPY MORNING GLORY SALAD
(Yum Pak Boong)

Morning glory, aka pak boong, is a tasty dark leafy green usually used in stir-fries. This is my favorite way to eat it—lightly battered with a light, tangy coconut dressing. Yes, it's deep-fried, but because it's a salad, that means it's healthy, right?

MAKES: 4 SERVINGS

Crispy Morning Glory

1½ qt (1.8 L) canola or other high-temperature cooking oil

7 oz (200 g) morning glory (stalk and leaves), cut into 3-inch (8-cm) pieces

2 cups (250 g) cornstarch

1 cup (125 g) all-purpose flour

1 tsp baking soda

1½ cups (360 ml) ice-cold water

Dressing

2 tbsp (30 ml) canola or other high-temperature oil

1 clove garlic, finely chopped

1–3 fresh Thai chilies, sliced thin

6 medium shrimp, peeled and deveined, sliced in half lengthwise and widthwise

1 shallot, finely sliced

¼ cup (60 ml) fresh lime juice

¼ cup (60 ml) fish sauce

¼ cup (55 g) palm sugar or brown sugar

2 tbsp (30 ml) full-fat coconut milk

Garnish

½ cup (60 g) thinly sliced red onion

¼ cup (30 g) peanuts, crushed

¼ cup (4 g) cilantro leaves

2 tbsp (10 g) store-bought fried shallots

To make the crispy morning glory, heat the oil in a 4-quart (3.8-L) Dutch oven to 375°F (190°C). While the oil is heating up, rinse the morning glory and drain in a colander until mostly dry. In a large bowl, whisk together the cornstarch, flour and baking soda. Measure out 1 cup (125 g) of the flour mixture and place it into a separate large bowl for dredging. Whisk the cold water into the remaining flour mixture until a thin pancake batter forms.

Dredge the cut and rinsed morning glory in the dredging flour. Place in the batter and coat until a thin layer of the batter forms. Fry the pieces in two to three batches until golden brown and crispy, 2 to 4 minutes for each batch. Drain the morning glory on paper towels or a rack for a minute, then transfer to a large serving plate.

To make the dressing, place a medium skillet over medium-high heat and let preheat for 1 minute. Swirl in the oil, then toss in the garlic, chilies and shrimp and sauté until the shrimp are just pink and opaque, 1 to 2 minutes, then turn off the heat. Using the residual heat of the pan, stir in the shallot, lime juice, fish sauce, sugar and coconut milk. Stir until the sugar is dissolved. Taste and adjust the seasoning if you'd like.

To serve, arrange the morning glory in the center of the serving plate. At the very last minute before eating, dress the salad with the dressing, keeping the shrimp and shallot pieces on top of the morning glory. Garnish with the red onion, crushed peanuts and cilantro, then sprinkle the store-bought fried shallots on top.

THAI YUM RICE SALAD (Khao Yum)

Besides being a very good way to utilize cooked rice, this is also one of those dishes that will satiate but is still light. I like to add grilled meat or seafood to this to make it a complete meal. If you can't find green mango, just use all Granny Smith apples.

MAKES: 4 SERVINGS

Dressing

1 shallot, finely sliced

1 clove garlic, finely chopped

1-2 fresh Thai chilies, thinly sliced

¼ cup (60 ml) fish sauce

¼ cup (55 g) palm sugar or brown sugar

¼ cup (60 ml) fresh lime juice

Salad

3 cups (600 g) cooked jasmine rice, chilled

2 cups (300 g) matchstick-cut green mango

1 cup (110 g) matchstick-cut Granny Smith apple

¼ cup (30 g) very thinly sliced red onion

½ cup (46 g) mint leaves

¼ cup (4 g) cilantro leaves

½ cup (56 g) toasted or roasted cashews

2 scallions, sliced on the bias

2 tbsp (5 g) dried shrimp, ground to a powder in a spice grinder

Make the dressing by combining all of the dressing ingredients, except the lime juice, in a small saucepan over medium heat. Stir until the sugar is dissolved and the mixture is combined. Transfer to a small bowl and stir in the lime juice. Place the dressing in the fridge and chill until ready to use.

Place the jasmine rice, mango and apple in a large mixing bowl. Gently toss for about 30 seconds to combine well without breaking the grains of rice. Add the dressing, onion, mint, cilantro and cashews to the bowl and continue to toss gently until combined.

Transfer to plates or a serving bowl and garnish with the scallions and dried shrimp powder.

BEAN SPROUTS STIR-FRIED WITH FRIED TOFU (Thua Ngok Pad Taohu)

Ali and I make this dish when we want a clean meal. It gives us the vegetables we want and need while the tofu also makes it filling. You can make this dish completely plant-based by using vegetarian oyster sauce.

MAKES: 2 SERVINGS

2 tbsp (30 ml) canola or other high-temperature cooking oil

1 (9-oz [255-g]) package fried tofu, cut into ¾-inch (2-cm) cubes

2 large cloves garlic, chopped

4 cups (500 g) mung bean sprouts or regular bean sprouts

3 scallions, cut into 2-inch (5-cm) pieces

2 tbsp (30 ml) oyster sauce

1 tbsp (15 ml) Thai soybean sauce

Dash of white pepper

Heat a medium skillet over high heat for about 1 minute. Swirl in the oil.

When you see wisps of white smoke, toss in the tofu and cook for about 30 seconds, until the tofu warms through and becomes crispy on the edges.

Stir in the garlic and sauté for about 20 seconds, until fragrant. Stir in the bean sprouts and scallions and stir-fry for about a minute, until they start to soften and are about half cooked through.

Add the oyster sauce and Thai soybean sauce and stir-fry for another minute until all ingredients are combined and well coated.

Taste and adjust any of the seasonings if you'd like. Stir in a dash of white pepper and serve hot.

MORNING GLORY ON FIRE

(Pak Boong Fai Dang)

This is a fun recipe where you load all the ingredients on a large platter or quarter sheet pan, get the wok screaming hot, then dump and stir-fry. In Thailand, there are vendors that cook this dish on one side of the street, then hurl it across the street and catch it with a plate that lands on your table. It's also called flying morning glory for that reason.

MAKES: 2 SERVINGS

½ lb (226 g) morning glory, washed, drained and cut into 3-inch (8-cm) pieces

2 Thai bird chilies, minced

2 cloves garlic, minced

1 tbsp (20 g) yellow soybean paste

1 tbsp (15 ml) light soy sauce

2 tbsp (30 ml) oyster sauce

2 tsp (10 g) white sugar

2 tbsp (30 ml) canola or other high-temperature cooking oil

Place the cut morning glory on a large platter. Then right on top, place the chilies, garlic, yellow bean paste, light soy sauce, oyster sauce and sugar. The idea is that once the pan is hot, you dump the morning glory and seasonings in all at one time and start cooking.

Heat a wok or large skillet over high heat for about 1 minute. This is one of the few times I do recommend a wok, about 12 to 14 inches (30 to 36 cm) wide. A large Dutch oven would be great for this dish, too. Add the oil to the pan.

When you see wisps of white smoke, carefully dump the morning glory and seasonings into the pan. It might sputter and pop, so be careful. Using two large spoons or large tongs, turn the contents of the pan over every 5 to 10 seconds, until the greens wilt by half and turn bright green, 3 to 4 minutes. Taste and adjust any of the seasonings if you'd like. Serve hot.

PLANT-BASED THAI

I'm so excited to share this chapter. It's something I had wanted to add to my first book but it didn't seem as timely or needed several years ago as it does now. This isn't a manifesto about going plant based, nor about being a vegetarian; it's about teaching the practical way to enjoy Thai food like so many do if they are plant based. It's about understanding ingredients and expanding your knowledge of creating flavor. There will be cooks that never touch this chapter and those that will cook only from it, then apply techniques learned to all the chapters! That's very exciting to me.

In addition, I truly believe that vegan food is delicious! A lot of cooks run from the "v" word, and it's really because most chefs don't know how to cook without meat. The simple fact is meat and meat products are naturally full of umami, so it's easy for anyone to make them delicious. Making vegetables, fruits and starches tasty is harder, but totally doable. It's about retraining your brain to think about flavors. Learning new sauce and flavor combinations is key. In many Thai dishes, we're replacing fish sauce with soy sauce or amino acid sauce and leaving out things like dried shrimp. Check out amino acid sauces if you are cooking more plant based. It may sound like a science experiment, but amino sauces are a great substitute for fish sauce and good for Asian dishes across the board. You will typically find bottles labeled coconut aminos or liquid aminos; a lot of grocery stores carry them now in the natural food section.

SPICY BASIL TOFU STIR-FRY
(Krapow Taohu)

This is one of the most popular Thai street foods. You can play around with the types of tofu to achieve different textures. Firm tofu packed in water, cut into a small dice, will give you a ground meat experience, while vacuum-packed tofu, thinly sliced, will eat more like sliced meat. Vegetarian oyster sauce exists only in the Chinese style, so don't be frustrated if you can't find Thai vegetarian oyster sauce. Also, don't be scared to substitute with Italian basil here if you can't find Thai basil.

MAKES: 4 SERVINGS

2 tbsp (30 ml) sweet soy sauce

2 tbsp (30 ml) vegetarian oyster sauce

3 tbsp (45 ml) Thai soybean sauce

1 tbsp (15 ml) vegan Thai sriracha

3 tbsp (45 ml) canola or other high-temperature cooking oil

3 cloves garlic, minced

1–3 fresh serrano or Thai chilies, sliced

1 lb (454 g) vacuum-packed tofu, cut into large dice

1 medium onion, sliced

1 small red bell pepper, sliced

1½ cups (9 g) Thai basil leaves, stripped from the stem

½ tsp white pepper

To make the sauce, combine the sweet soy sauce, vegetarian oyster sauce, soybean sauce, and sriracha in a small bowl and set aside.

Heat a wok or large skillet over high heat and add the oil. When you see the first wisp of white smoke, add the garlic, chilies and tofu. Cook until the garlic starts to brown, about 30 seconds.

Stir in the onion and bell pepper and stir-fry for about 1 minute. Add the reserved sauce to the wok and combine the ingredients thoroughly for about 1 minute. Add the Thai basil leaves and cook until the tofu is thoroughly cooked and the onion is slightly tender. Finish with the white pepper and serve.

VEGAN PAD SEE EW (Pad See Ew Jay)

Traditional Thai monks are plant-based eaters, so vegan dishes are nothing new to Thai food. The lack of eggs in this version of pad see ew will make the pan a little sticky, so get your pan very hot and keep the food moving. Don't be scared to scrape bits off the pan as the tofu and noodles are browning so they don't burn.

MAKES: 4 SERVINGS

3 tbsp (45 ml) Chinese sweet soy sauce

1 tbsp (15 ml) vegetarian oyster sauce

3 tbsp (45 ml) vegetarian fish sauce or Thai soybean sauce

1 tbsp (15 g) white sugar

3 tbsp (45 ml) canola or other high-temperature cooking oil

4 oz (112 g) firm, unseasoned vacuum-packed tofu, sliced thin

2 cloves garlic, minced

1½ cups (150 g) broccoli florets

4 cups (480 g) fresh rice noodles (store-bought or homemade from page 56)

½ tsp white pepper

Combine the Chinese sweet soy sauce, vegetarian oyster sauce, vegetarian fish sauce and sugar in a small bowl, mixing well to dissolve the sugar. Set aside.

Heat the oil over high heat in a large skillet for about 1 minute. When you see the first wisps of white smoke, add the tofu and garlic and sauté for about 1 minute, or until the exterior of the tofu is lightly browned on the edges. Make sure to scrape any bits off the pan before they burn.

Add the broccoli and noodles, tossing them constantly until the edges of the noodles begin to brown and the broccoli starts to turn dark green, 1 to 2 minutes.

Add the sauce and stir constantly to combine for about 3 minutes, until the noodles soak up the sauce and start to crisp slightly on the edges.

Sprinkle with white pepper and serve immediately.

VEGAN COCONUT GALANGA SOUP
(Tom Kha Jay)

Making Thai soups plant based is easy. A lot of people look down on instant vegetable bases and concentrates, but they are packed with umami and flavor. They all vary slightly in salt level so you might need to dial in your amounts either to back down the saltiness or to ramp up the amount of the base to get more savory and saltiness.

MAKES: 4 SERVINGS, ABOUT 2 CUPS (480 ML) EACH

8 cups (1.9 L) cold water

3 oz (85 g) vegetable base paste like Knorr or Minor's

3–5 thin slices galanga

1 stalk lemongrass, tough outer leaves discarded, sliced thinly on the bias

2 kaffir lime leaves, folded in half and twisted

1–3 fresh Thai chilies, split

6 oz (170 g) medium firmness tofu in water, drained and cut into 1-inch (3-cm) cubes

1 (15-oz [425-g]) can straw mushrooms, drained

1 cup (90 g) chopped cabbage

1 cup (240 ml) full-fat coconut milk

1½ tbsp (22 ml) white vinegar

1 tbsp (15 ml) fresh lime juice

1½ tsp (7 g) kosher salt

1½ tbsp (23 g) white sugar

Cilantro leaves, for garnish

Pour the water into a 4-quart (3.8-L) pot over high heat. Bring the water to a boil and whisk in the vegetable base until it is completely dissolved. Reduce the heat to a simmer and place the pieces of galanga, lemongrass, lime leaves and chilies into the pot. Simmer for 30 minutes to make the stock.

To finish the soup, stir in the tofu, mushrooms and cabbage and cook until the cabbage softens, about 2 minutes.

Stir in the coconut milk, vinegar, lime juice, salt and sugar. Continue stirring until the sugar is dissolved. Taste and adjust any of the flavors if you'd like, then garnish with the cilantro leaves and serve.

VEGAN YELLOW CURRY (Gang Leung Jay)

Most yellow curries don't contain shrimp paste as other types do. But read your labels closely to make sure shrimp paste isn't included. You can use this recipe and substitute your favorite kind of curry paste—or even combinations of different curry pastes—and other types of vegetables and proteins. Vegetarian fish sauce is going to give you a better flavor than regular soy sauce here. It's worth trying to find it online or in an Asian market.

MAKES: 4 SERVINGS

2 (13-oz [384-ml]) cans full-fat coconut milk, with 3 tbsp (45 ml) of the cream separated out

2–3 tbsp (32–48 g) vegetarian yellow curry paste

2 kaffir lime leaves, cut into a fine chiffonade

½ cup (60 g) thinly sliced brown onion

½ cup (20 g) roughly chopped Thai sweet basil (whole, including stems)

1 lb (454 g) firm tofu, sliced into ¼-inch (6-mm)–thick tiles

1 cup (260 g) canned sliced bamboo shoots

½ cup (95 g) sliced red bell pepper

2 tsp (10 ml) vegetarian fish sauce

½ tsp kosher salt

1 tsp tamarind concentrate

1 tsp palm sugar or brown sugar

Cooked jasmine rice, for serving (optional)

In a medium saucepan, warm the 3 tablespoons (45 ml) of thick coconut cream over high heat for about 1 minute. When the cream starts to sizzle, stir the curry paste into the cream as if you were building a roux. Add the lime leaves. Stir-fry the paste for about 1 minute, until the paste starts to thicken, dry out and become fragrant. If the curry starts to sputter, add a small amount of coconut milk to keep the paste moving. Cook the paste until it has the consistency of peanut butter.

Stir in the onion, basil and remaining coconut milk. Heat until you reach a full rolling boil. Allow the curry to boil for 10 to 15 minutes, or until it reduces by about one-quarter and coats the back of a wooden spoon.

Reduce the heat to a simmer. Add the tofu, bamboo shoots, red bell pepper, vegetarian fish sauce, salt, tamarind concentrate and palm sugar. Let this simmer for about 5 more minutes or until the vegetables are cooked. Serve hot over cooked rice.

VEGAN PAD THAI (Pad Thai Jay)

Four years ago, my plant-based friends always gave me a hard time because I had never published a vegan Pad Thai recipe. I would sit in the kitchen and doctor a recipe for my plant-based guests, and at last I've thoughtfully tested it and put it on paper. I'm glad and honored to finally share this recipe here with you.

MAKES: 4 SERVINGS

Noodles

8 oz (227 g) dry Pad Thai noodles (dry Chantaboon rice stick)

Sauce

3 tbsp (45 ml) vegetarian fish sauce or Thai soybean sauce

1 tbsp (15 ml) tamarind concentrate

1 tbsp (15 ml) fresh lime juice

2 tsp (10 ml) unseasoned rice vinegar

¼ cup (55 g) palm sugar, brown sugar or white sugar

¼ cup (60 ml) water

Pad Thai

3 tbsp (45 ml) canola or other high-temperature cooking oil

3 cloves garlic, roughly chopped

½ cup (125 g) diced savory baked tofu

1½ tbsp (15 g) packaged minced sweet pickled turnip

2 tbsp (14 g) paprika (optional)

3–4 scallions, cut into 2-inch (5-cm) pieces on the bias

¼ cup (30 g) chopped dry-roasted peanuts, divided

1 cup (125 g) bean sprouts

Soak the dry noodles in a large bowl of warm (90°F [32°C]) water for about 1 hour. The noodles will start to absorb water, loosen up and be ready for the pan. After they've soaked, drain and set aside. If using fresh noodles, you can just open the package and add them to the pan at the appropriate time.

To make the sauce, combine the vegetarian fish sauce or Thai soybean sauce, tamarind concentrate, lime juice, unseasoned rice vinegar, palm sugar and water in a small bowl. Stir well until the sugar dissolves. Set aside.

Heat a skillet or wok over high heat for about 1 minute until the pan gets hot. Add the oil and swirl to coat the pan completely. When the pan just starts to smoke, add the garlic and stir for about 5 seconds. Add the tofu and pickled turnip and stir-fry until they begin to get fragrant, about 1 minute.

Add the drained noodles and cook for 2 to 3 minutes, until soft. Add the sauce mixture and paprika, if using, and fold everything together until the paprika evenly colors the noodles and all the liquid is absorbed, about 2 minutes.

Place the scallions in the center of the noodles, and then spoon some noodles over the scallions to cover and let them steam for 30 seconds. Stir in 3 tablespoons (23 g) of the peanuts. Transfer to a serving plate and garnish with the bean sprouts and remaining peanuts.

VEGAN DRUNKEN NOODLES
(Pad Kee Mow Jay)

When I was cooking in Las Vegas, the owner of the hotel became plant-based and asked every restaurant to create vegan versions of their most popular dishes, which for me was drunken noodles. It was a really nice push to try to make a plant-based version of such an iconic dish. The key here is finding a vegetarian oyster-flavored sauce for its flavor balance and thickness.

MAKES: 2 SERVINGS

Sauce

5 tbsp (75 ml) Chinese sweet soy sauce

3 tbsp (45 ml) vegetarian oyster sauce

3 tbsp (45 ml) vegetarian fish sauce or Thai soybean sauce

2 tbsp (30 g) white sugar

2 tsp (10 ml) vegan sriracha

2 tsp (10 g) minced garlic

6–8 Thai basil leaves, cut chiffonade

Drunken Noodles

3 tbsp (45 ml) canola or other high-temperature cooking oil

2–3 cloves garlic, minced

1–2 serrano chilies, sliced thin

5 oz (145 g) extra-firm tofu in water, drained and sliced into 1-inch (3-cm) cubes

½ medium white onion, sliced

3–4 cups (360–480 g) fresh rice noodles (store-bought or homemade from page 56), separated

½ cup (100 g) grape tomatoes, halved

1 cup (24 g) Thai basil leaves, loosely packed

Combine the sauce ingredients in a small bowl, whisking well to dissolve the sugar, then set it aside.

Heat the oil over medium-high heat in a medium-sized sauté pan. At the first wisp of white smoke, add the garlic and serrano chilies and sauté until the garlic is light brown. Stir in the diced tofu and onion slices, folding constantly until the tofu starts to brown, 1 to 2 minutes.

Add the fresh rice noodles and sauté until the noodles are soft and slightly browned on the edges, about 2 minutes.

Add the sauce, tomatoes and basil. Toss them together to combine for 3 to 5 minutes. Make sure the noodles completely absorb the sauce. Divide between two plates and serve hot.

THAI VEGAN FRIED RICE (Khao Pad Jay)

This is a plant-based version of a street-style Thai fried rice. Leftover cold rice is the better rice for this recipe because you don't have the non-stick assistance of using eggs. You might have to bump up the oil a little bit to keep the rice from sticking to the pan.

MAKES: 4 SERVINGS

3 tbsp (45 ml) canola or other high-temperature cooking oil

5 oz (142 g) savory baked tofu, medium dice

2 stalks Chinese broccoli, leaves torn into large pieces and stalks sliced thin

2 large cloves garlic, minced

¼ medium brown onion, sliced

3 cups (480 g) cooked and chilled Thai jasmine rice

1 tsp white sugar

Kosher salt

1½ tbsp (25 ml) vegetarian fish sauce or Thai soybean sauce

1 medium Roma tomato, cut into 6 pieces lengthwise

½ tsp white pepper

2 scallions, sliced thin

Heat a heavy 9- to 11-inch (23- to 28-cm) pan over high heat for about 1 minute to preheat. Swirl in the oil, making sure it evenly coats the whole pan. When you see a wisp of white smoke, stir in the tofu and stir-fry for about 1 minute, until warmed through.

Clear some space in the pan by moving the tofu to the side. Stir in the Chinese broccoli, garlic and onion and cook for about 30 seconds, until the broccoli leaves wilt and the onion starts to soften. Add the rice and gently smash it flat into the pan without breaking the grains. Continue to fold and smash for about a minute until the rice clumps loosen, combine with the rest of the ingredients and warm up.

Sprinkle in the sugar, salt and vegetarian fish sauce or Thai soybean sauce. Keep doing the circular smash and fold motion until all the seasonings are evenly distributed and the rice is hot and toasty, 1 to 2 minutes. Toss in the tomato pieces, white pepper and scallions and stir to incorporate and heat for another minute. Enjoy!

Pro Tip: Cold day-old rice from the fridge works best. Spray down the cold rice with some pan spray; that will keep the rice from sticking to the pan without having to use too much oil.

VEGAN TOFU LARB (Taohu Lap)

For this dish, it's important to use medium tofu in water. Medium tofu crumbles perfectly and mimics ground meat. If you find the tofu is a little too soft, you can press out excess moisture in a colander. Prelubricating the tofu with a little bit of oil also keeps it from sticking to the pan. Larb is a spicy acidic salad from the northeast of Thailand usually made with ground meat. It's great alone or as a protein side with crunchy cold vegetables.

MAKES: 4–6 SERVINGS

1½ lb (680 g) medium tofu in water, drained

1 tbsp (15 ml) tamarind concentrate

2 tbsp (30 ml) canola or other high-temperature cooking oil

3 cloves garlic, minced

1 large shallot, thinly sliced

¼ cup (60 ml) vegetarian fish sauce or Thai soybean sauce

½ cup (120 ml) fresh lime juice

½ cup (110 g) palm sugar or brown sugar

1–2 tsp Thai chili powder

½ cup (46 g) mint leaves

½ red onion, thinly sliced

¼ cup (55 g) roasted rice powder (see Pro Tip)

3–4 scallions, chopped

Carrot sticks, 4–5 inches (10–13 cm) long, for serving

Long beans or other green beans, 4–5 inches (10–13 cm) long, for serving

Lettuce leaves, in 4–5-inch (10–13-cm) pieces, for serving

Green cabbage, in 4–5-inch (10–13-cm) pieces, for serving

Prepare the tofu by slicing it into ¼-inch (6-mm) tiles, then cut the tiles into ¼-inch (6-mm) slices, then finally cut the slices into a fine dice. Place the diced tofu in a medium-sized bowl. Stir the tamarind concentrate into the diced tofu and let it stand for 15 minutes.

Heat a medium-sized pan over high heat and swirl in the oil. When you see the first wisps of white smoke, add the garlic and shallot and sauté for about 1 minute, until the shallot is translucent and the garlic is fragrant. Fold in the tofu and stir-fry until heated through, about 2 minutes. If any liquid is released, either drain it from the pan or continue cooking to reduce it so it does not dilute the seasonings.

Turn off the heat, then stir in the vegetarian fish sauce, lime juice, sugar and chili powder and mix well. Adjust the flavors as necessary to your taste. Fold in the mint, red onion, roasted rice powder and scallions until well combined.

Serve with carrot sticks, long beans, lettuce and cabbage.

Pro Tip: Roasted rice powder is a fun condiment. It adds a quintessential nutty, smoky crunch to larb as well as other dishes. It also soaks up the dressing and binds it to the dish, upping the flavor. Look for it at an Asian market, or make it at home. This homemade version makes ½ cup (90 g). Place ½ cup (90 g) dry Thai sticky rice in a medium dry pan over medium-high heat. When the pan starts to heat up and you smell the rice toasting, stir or pan-flip the rice every 20 seconds. If the rice seems like it's browning too fast, reduce the heat to low. Cook for 5 to 10 minutes, until the rice is golden brown. Remove the pan from the heat and allow the rice to cool. Transfer the cooled rice to a spice grinder and pulse until it's sandy in texture.

STIR-FRIED CHINESE BROCCOLI (Pad Khana)

This is a classic street food dish traditionally eaten over jasmine rice with meat and a fried egg, but for a plant-based version, the Chinese broccoli shines all on its own. It's the perfect combination of healthy and rich, balanced flavors. You can ramp up the heat with more chilies. Substitute American broccoli crowns if you can't find Chinese broccoli.

MAKES: 2 SERVINGS

1 lb (454 g) Chinese broccoli, leaves cut into 2-inch (5-cm) pieces and stems sliced on the bias 1 inch (3 cm) long by ½ inch (13 mm) wide

½ cup (120 ml) water

1 tbsp (15 ml) canola or other high-temperature cooking oil

2 large cloves garlic, chopped

1–2 Thai bird chilies, cut into thin slices

¼ cup (9 g) dried Thai chilies or chilies de arbol

2 tbsp (30 ml) vegetarian oyster sauce

2 tsp (10 ml) Thai soybean sauce

1 tsp white sugar

Dash of white pepper to taste

Cooked jasmine rice, for serving

Place the trimmed and cut Chinese broccoli into a large glass bowl, pour in the water and seal it tightly with plastic wrap. Microwave on high for 90 seconds. Remove the plastic wrap, drain and set aside.

Heat a medium skillet over high heat for about 1 minute. Swirl in the oil and wait until you see wisps of white smoke. BEWARE of spicy smoke in the next step. Stir in the garlic, fresh chilies and dried chilies and sauté until fragrant, about 20 seconds.

Stir in the Chinese broccoli and stir-fry for about 30 seconds, until the edges get smoky and crispy and the broccoli cooks through. Add the oyster sauce, soybean sauce and sugar and stir-fry for about 30 seconds, until the ingredients are well combined and well coated in the sauce. Taste and adjust any of the seasonings if you'd like. Stir in a dash of white pepper and serve hot over rice.

TOFU SATAY (Taohu Satay)

Addictive and easy to make, these tofu satays are perfect for any gathering or for grilling weather. Make sure your curry paste does not contain shrimp for this recipe. Also make sure to use firm tofu in water so the tofu does not fall apart. You can make these ahead of time and hold them in the fridge before cooking for up to a week.

MAKES: 10–12 SKEWERS

2 tsp (14 g) red curry paste (check that it's shrimp-free)

1 tbsp (6 g) curry powder

½ tbsp (5 g) ground black pepper

1 tbsp (15 g) kosher salt

1 tbsp (15 g) white sugar

1 tsp garlic powder, or more to taste

½ cup (120 ml) full-fat coconut milk

2 lb (907 g) firm tofu in water

10–15 (6-inch [15-cm]) bamboo skewers, soaked

Canola or other high-temperature cooking oil, or pan spray

Vegan Peanut Sauce (page 185), for serving

To make the marinade, combine the curry paste, curry powder, pepper, salt, sugar, garlic powder and coconut milk in a medium-sized bowl.

Remove the tofu blocks from their packages, drain well and set on paper towels for 5 to 10 minutes to dry out. Slice the blocks into 1½-inch (4-cm)–wide bricks, then into 1½-inch (4-cm) squares and then into ¼-inch (6-mm)-thick slices. Add the pieces to the marinade and massage to coat them evenly.

Thread the tofu tiles onto the bamboo skewers, leaving 2 inches (5 cm) at the bottom of each skewer. You can cook the skewers immediately or marinate them overnight for better flavor and texture.

Heat a grill or griddle to high and preheat for at least 5 minutes. Rub a little oil on the grill or spray with pan spray. Grill the tofu for 2 to 3 minutes on the first side or until you get nice grill marks. Flip and cook for another 2 to 3 minutes, or until marked and heated through.

NORTHERN THAI EGGPLANT AND CHILI DIP (Nam Prik Noom)

Chili dips are an excellent way to incorporate vegetables, chilies and proteins into an easy-to-eat dish. They hold for long periods of time, are very portable and provide a nutritionally packed quick meal. If you love spicy food, this is the perfect dip for you. For the plant-based version of this classic dish, we are using vegetarian fish sauce (or use Thai soybean sauce if you can't find it), leaving out the traditional 1 teaspoon of Thai shrimp paste and using puffed rice chips for savory crunch instead of traditional pork rinds.

MAKES: 2 SERVINGS

10–15 (6-inch [15-cm]) bamboo skewers, soaked

5 fresh Thai green chilies

3 cloves garlic, peeled

3 shallots, peeled

2 small Chinese eggplants, with peel

3 Anaheim chili peppers, with peel

Canola or other high-temperature cooking oil, for brushing

2½ tbsp (38 ml) vegetarian fish sauce

Puffed rice chips

1 cucumber, bias sliced

6 oz (170 g) fresh green beans or long beans, cut into 3-inch (8-cm) pieces

Thai Sticky Rice (page 80)

Similar to making mini-kabobs, separately skewer the Thai chilies, garlic, shallots, eggplants and Anaheim chilies. Preheat a grill pan on high for about 2 minutes. Lightly oil the chilies, garlic, shallots and vegetables, then place the skewers on the grill pan. Cook for 2 to 3 minutes on each side until the skins char, similar to roasting bell peppers. You want them blackened and the flesh very tender. Place the roasted vegetables in a bowl and cover with plastic wrap to help steam the skins off. Peel the peppers and remove the seeds. Scrape off the charred skin from the eggplant. Cut the eggplants into a rough, large dice to make them easier to process.

Transfer the Thai chilies, garlic and shallots to a food processor. Run the machine, stopping and scraping down the sides, then process again until the mixture is broken down into small pieces. Next, add the eggplant, Anaheim chilies and vegetarian fish sauce. Pulse in short bursts to combine but maintain some texture in the dish. Taste and adjust the seasoning if you'd like. Serve with the puffed rice chips, cucumber, long beans and sticky rice.

VEGAN PEANUT SAUCE

(Nam Jim Satay Jay)

This version of the popular sauce is plant based, without sacrificing any of the delicious flavor. The main change is the substitution of fish sauce, where you have two good options. It's worth searching for vegan fish sauce on the web. If you can't find it, Thai soybean sauce makes it just a little darker and less salty.

MAKES: 4 SERVINGS

2 tbsp (30 ml) canola or other high-temperature cooking oil

1 tbsp (21 g) red curry paste (check that it is shrimp-free), or more to taste

2 cups (480 ml) full-fat coconut milk

2 tbsp (30 g) peanut butter (chunky or smooth), or more to taste

1 tsp kosher salt

1 tbsp (15 ml) vegetarian fish sauce or Thai soybean sauce

½ tsp unseasoned rice vinegar

2 tbsp (30 g) white sugar, or more to taste

Heat the oil in a small saucepan over high heat. When hot, add the curry paste and stir-fry for about 1 minute or until it becomes very fragrant and thick. Stir in the coconut milk and bring it to a boil; cook for 2 minutes while constantly stirring. Be careful not to let it boil over.

Add the peanut butter and salt, stirring constantly until the sauce begins to thicken and come together, about 2 to 3 minutes. Reduce the heat to a simmer and add the vegetarian fish sauce, unseasoned rice vinegar and sugar. Cook the sauce for 1 minute more, then remove it from the heat. An oily film will rise to the top; skim it off if you wish. You can serve the sauce immediately or keep it in the fridge for up to a month.

KANOM WAN
SWEET THAI LIFE

There cannot be any sweet without a hint of salt. This is what every Thai chef preaches. Thai desserts are a wonderful world of coconuts, palm sugar, pandan leaf, fruit and rice. The fundamentals of custard, cake and sugar are universal, but Thai chefs are masters at desserts with a light touch. I say that because most Thai desserts are not cloyingly sweet but balance natural flavors with essential oils and delicate textures. There's also a beautiful interplay with nature. Many desserts don't just use jasmine essence but also strive to look like flowers. Don't get me wrong, I love chocolate, pastries and ice cream, but I love the delicate approach of Thai desserts. You will learn and appreciate that nature can be sweet and crave-worthy. Big props to Ali for creating a lot of these recipes by working with Thai chefs, dessert makers and my mom, Mary. This was a delicious chapter to develop and write as a family.

STEAMED COCONUT CUSTARD IN KABOCHA SQUASH (Faktong Sangkaya)

This is a uniquely Thai dessert made by filling a sweet kabocha squash with coconut custard then steaming it whole. The custard solidifies in the squash, and when cooled, you can make a slice that perfectly shows off the custard.

MAKES: 4 SERVINGS

1 kabocha squash

6 eggs

1¼ cups (275 g) palm sugar or brown sugar (see Pro Tip)

3 tbsp (24 g) flour

1 tsp kosher salt

2 pandan leaves

1 cup (240 ml) full-fat coconut milk

Pro Tip: Palm sugar viscosity depends on how old it is. Fresh is soft and pliable and dry is hard like dried brown sugar. The soft fresh sugar works into the eggs and custard easily. But if you end up with the dry stuff, don't fret. You can run the dry hard palm sugar in a food processor until it granulates and it will be easier to use. You can substitute palm sugar with light brown sugar as well.

Start by hollowing out the kabocha squash. Cut a round or square hole off the top, 1 to 2 inches (3 to 5 cm) around the stem. Try to keep the stem intact in case you want to use it as a cover. Loosen the seeds with a fork first, then scoop them out with a spoon. When the seeds have been removed, it's time to make the custard.

To make the custard, crack the eggs into a large bowl. Add the palm sugar, flour, salt, pandan leaves and coconut milk. The old-school way to make this is to use your hands to mix the ingredients. It works best because your hands can squish the pandan leaves, releasing the essential oils and breaking up the yolks. This process is called "kayum" in Thai. If you want to forgo using your hands in the egg mixture, you can beat the custard with a hand mixer or stand mixer and break up the pandan with your hands for a few minutes until fragrant. Strain the mixture into a bowl through a strainer that isn't too fine.

Set up a steamer large enough to accommodate the whole kabocha squash. Add 5 to 6 inches (13 to 15 cm) of water into the steamer base and bring it to a boil. You can either use a funnel or pour the custard into a 4-cup (960-ml) pourable measuring cup. Place the squash into the steamer basket then place over the steamer base. Pour the custard into the squash until it just fills the squash, leaving about ½ inch (13 mm) of space at the top. Place the top of the squash that you cut out as a "lid" on the squash and steam on medium steam for 30 to 40 minutes, or until a skewer pulls out clean from the center of the custard, similar to checking a cake for doneness. Remove the steamer from the heat and allow the squash to cool to room temperature, about 20 minutes. When cool, slice into 3-inch (8-cm) wedges.

You can serve this dish warm or allow it to set in the fridge for up to 2 days. Note that you can eat the squash and even the tender skin.

SWEET COCONUT MILK PANCAKES (Kanom Krok)

These are little half-moon–shaped mini coconut fritters that are cooked in metal pans that resemble Dutch pancake pans. You can find aebleskiver or Japanese takoyaki pans on the Internet or at some restaurant supply stores.

MAKES: 4 SERVINGS

Base Layer

¼ cup (50 g) white sugar

½ tsp kosher salt

⅔ cup (100 g) white rice flour (not glutinous or sticky rice flour)

½ tbsp (4 g) all-purpose flour

¾ cup (180 ml) full-fat coconut milk

1 cup (240 ml) water

Top Layer

½ cup (100 g) white sugar

½ tsp kosher salt

¾ cup (180 ml) full-fat coconut milk

To make the base layer, combine the sugar, salt, rice flour, all-purpose flour, coconut milk and water in a medium bowl and whisk until all ingredients are thoroughly combined. Set aside.

To make the top layer, combine the ingredients in a small saucepan over medium heat and bring to a simmer. Reduce the heat to low and cook the ingredients, constantly stirring, until they have combined.

To cook, heat an aebleskiver or takoyaki pan to 380°F (195°C). Spray each dimple with pan spray or use a wadded-up paper towel dipped in oil to coat. Pour the bottom layer mixture into each hole and fill three-quarters full. Let the edges brown slightly and set, about 30 seconds. Now pour the top layer over the bottom layer until it's level with the pan. Place a lid on top and let it cook for about 2 minutes or until the fritter completely sets, is brown on the bottom and bubbly on top. Using a soup spoon or Chinese soup spoon, scoop out the fritters and transfer to a cooling rack to let rest before serving.

The trick to keeping the shape is to take one of the fritters that have cooked faster and set them upside down on top of the ones that haven't finished cooking. This allows for the ones that have finished to crisp up so it can hold the weight of the two halves on the cooling rack.

THAI CREPES WITH PANDAN CREAM (Khanom Tokyo)

This dessert eats like mini sweet pancakes filled with custard. The cream is infused with pandan, which makes it fun and green. The crepe batter is made with coconut milk and is pleasantly spongy— the perfect vessel to complement the sweet custard.

MAKES: 2 SERVINGS

Crepe Batter

2 eggs

½ cup (100 g) white sugar

1 cup (125 g) flour

½ tsp baking soda

¾ cup (180 ml) milk

Pandan Cream

15 pandan leaves, roughly chopped (or pandan extract)

1 cup (240 ml) water

1 cup plus 2 tbsp (270 ml) full-fat coconut milk

4 egg yolks

½ cup (120 ml) sweetened condensed milk

6½ tbsp (52 g) cornstarch

½ cup (100 g) white sugar

½ tsp kosher salt

In a large bowl, whisk all the crepe batter ingredients together until well combined and smooth. Cover and refrigerate for 1 hour.

In a blender, puree the pandan leaves and the water. Strain the puree until you have ½ cup plus 2 tablespoons (150 ml) of pandan water. You can also use two to four drops of pandan extract instead, skipping this step.

In a bowl, whisk the coconut milk and egg yolks. One ingredient at a time, whisk in the sweetened condensed milk, cornstarch, sugar and salt; whisk until the sugar dissolves a bit. Add the pandan water and stir until combined. Cook the pandan cream over a double boiler, stirring constantly, until thickened, 5 to 7 minutes (times may vary). Remove the double boiler from the heat and continue to stir while the pandan cream cools. When it has cooled, transfer it into a pastry bag or place plastic wrap directly onto the surface of the cream (so a skin does not form) and place it in the refrigerator to thicken more, about 20 minutes.

To make the crepes, drop large spoonfuls of the crepe batter onto a griddle set to 325°F (165°C) or a pan over medium-high heat. Use the back of the spoon to spread the batter evenly in a circular motion to create the circular shape of the crepes. When most of the bubbles in the batter have popped and the bottom of the crepe is golden brown, pipe the pandan cream in a line across each crepe (or drop a spoonful in the center). Using a spatula to lift the edge of the crepe, gently roll the crepe around the pandan cream. Transfer to a serving plate and repeat with the rest of the crepe batter and pandan cream. Serve immediately.

COCONUT STICKY RICE
WITH MANGO (Khao Neow Mamuang)

Mangos are available almost all year long in Thailand, and there is never a shortage of rice. Here is a sinful dessert that joins the two. I know rice is rarely considered a dessert food, but this is a delicious treat. Coconut sticky rice can be eaten with any fruit and is also great by itself. Thai sweet rice, not jasmine, is used to make this dish. What makes the rice stick together is its high starch content. Sweet rice is steamed instead of simmered.

This is a special dessert, and like all things that taste sinful, it is to be enjoyed in moderation. Manila mangos are in season in the United States for 3 to 4 months out of the year, but their extra sweetness and soft texture make them a perfect accompaniment to the coconut sticky rice, so get them when you can.

MAKES: 4–6 SERVINGS

3 cups (540 g) dry Thai sweet rice

2 cups (480 ml) full-fat coconut milk

1–1½ cups (200–300 g) white sugar

1 tsp kosher salt

4 Manila mangoes, sliced

Add the sweet rice to a bowl and cover with water. Soak for at least 3 hours, preferably overnight.

Transfer the soaked rice to a bamboo basket. The rice should sit on the bottom of the basket. Add 4 cups (960 ml) of water to a steamer pot. Heat the water over high heat until it's boiling.

Insert the basket into the pot, cover it and cook for 10 minutes. Flip the rice once and let it steam for another 10 minutes. Pour the rice into a large metal or glass bowl.

Heat the coconut milk, sugar and salt in a small saucepan until simmering, then remove the pan from the heat. Reserve ¼ cup (60 ml) of the mixture and fold the remaining coconut sauce into the rice. Cover the rice for 30 minutes.

Serve with the mangoes or any fruit in season. Drizzle the remaining coconut milk mixture over the top before serving.

THAI ICED TEA (Cha Nom Yen)

Thai tea is very similar to Indian chai tea. The base is black tea with spices like vanilla, cloves and cardamom added. It's supposed to be super sweet and served over a ton of ice, but by making it at home, you can control the amount of sweetness. You can find packaged Thai tea mix at Asian markets or on the Internet with a few clicks. It's so much easier than making it on your own.

MAKES: 2 SERVINGS

4 cups (960 ml) water

½ cup (60 g) packaged Thai tea mix

1 cup (200 g) white sugar

3–4 tbsp (45–60 ml) half-and-half

Bring the water to a boil in a medium saucepan. Stir in the Thai tea mix. Simmer it over medium-low heat for about 20 minutes. Stir in the sugar, to taste. Strain the tea through a sieve lined with cheesecloth or a clean tea towel. Chill it in the fridge for a few hours. It will keep, refrigerated, for up to 2 weeks.

When ready to serve, fill two tall glasses with ice. Pour the tea over the ice, leaving about ½ inch (13 mm) of room at the top. Top with the half-and-half and insert a straw. Use the straw to mix in the half-and-half thoroughly before drinking.

THAI ICED COFFEE (Cafe Yen)

Legend has it that what gives Thai coffee its distinctive nutty flavor is tamarind roasted with the coffee. I'm not sure how true that is, but I love Thai coffee because it's strong without being too bitter. Some street vendors substitute evaporated or condensed milk for the half-and-half. I personally like using the half-and-half; it's a cleaner flavor. You can also use this recipe for an ice cream base.

MAKES: 2 SERVINGS

4 cups (960 ml) water

¼ cup (26 g) packaged Thai coffee mix

1 cup (200 g) white sugar, or to taste

3 tbsp (45 ml) half-and-half

Bring the water to a boil in a medium saucepan. Stir in the Thai coffee mix. Simmer it over medium-low heat for about 20 minutes. Stir in the sugar, to taste. Strain the coffee through a sieve lined with cheesecloth or a clean tea towel. Chill it in the fridge for a few hours; you can hold it for up to 2 weeks in the fridge.

When ready to serve, fill two tall glasses with ice. Pour the coffee over the ice, leaving about ½ inch (13 mm) of room at the top. Top with the half-and-half and insert a straw. Use the straw to mix in the half-and-half thoroughly before drinking.

SAUCES, DIPS & CONDIMENTS

Thai cuisine is one of the few Asian cuisines that encourages you to finish your dish with hot, sour, salty, sweet or savory touches. My Chinese grandmother would give you the stink-eye if you dared pour soy sauce on anything she cooked. Thai grandmothers, on the other hand, would bring condiment caddies, chilies and various dips for all dishes. The function of sauces, dips and condiments in Thai cuisine is all about personalization. There is a standing belief that all diners have different preferences. I like spicy and sweet so I might jazz up my dishes with a pinch of sugar and dried chili flakes. Ali likes acid and salt so she'll reach for serrano chilies in vinegar or fish sauce. The world of condiments and sauces in Thai food is a fun and adventurous one. So, it's time for you to Choose Your Own Adventure!

THAI PEANUT SAUCE (Nam Jim Satay)

Peanut sauce is the traditional accompaniment to satays, but I know so many people that eat it on everything. While it's also eaten in Indonesia, the Thai version is creamier and sweeter. You can thin the sauce out and make a peanut dressing by adding unseasoned rice vinegar.

MAKES: 2½ CUPS (600 ML)

2 tbsp (30 ml) canola or other high-temperature cooking oil

1 tbsp (21 g) red curry paste, or more to taste

2 cups (480 ml) full-fat coconut milk

2 tbsp (32 g) peanut butter (either chunky or smooth), or more to taste

2 tbsp (30 ml) fish sauce

½ tsp unseasoned rice vinegar

2 tbsp (30 g) white sugar, or more to taste

Heat the oil in a small saucepan over high heat. When hot, stir-fry the curry paste for about a minute or until very fragrant and thick.

Stir in the coconut milk, then bring it to a boil and cook for 2 minutes while constantly stirring. Be careful not to let it boil over. Add the peanut butter and stir constantly until the sauce begins to thicken and come together, 2 to 3 minutes.

Reduce the heat to a simmer and add the fish sauce, unseasoned rice vinegar and sugar. Cook the sauce for 1 minute more, then remove it from the heat. An oily film will rise to the top; skim it off if you wish. You can serve the sauce immediately, or keep it in the fridge for up to a month.

GRANDMA'S EVERYTHING DIPPING SAUCE

This was the dipping sauce my grandmother would make for her pan-fried pot stickers. To this day, the flavors remind me of her cooking. It's one of those sauces that is so simple yet perfect. I've made it many times in my professional career, and it constantly amazes and bewilders all the chefs who have tried it. Now it's yours to pass on and impress with.

MAKES: ¾ CUP (180 ML)

¼ cup (60 ml) soy sauce

¼ cup (60 ml) Thai sriracha

¼ cup (50 g) white sugar

Combine the ingredients in a small bowl and whisk together until the sugar is dissolved.

FISH SAUCE WITH CHILIES
(Prik Nam Pla)

This is the most common Thai chili condiment in all Thai restaurants and homes. It's easy to make and will hold in the fridge for about a week. A little goes a long way, so sprinkle a few drops on whatever you are eating.

MAKES: ¾ CUP (180 ML)

3 cloves garlic, finely minced

1–2 Thai bird chilies, sliced into ⅛-inch (3-mm) rounds

½ cup (120 ml) fresh lime juice

¼ cup (60 ml) fish sauce

2 tsp (30 g) white or palm sugar

Mix the minced garlic, Thai bird chilies, lime juice, fish sauce and sugar in a bowl. Taste and adjust for your desired level of spice by adding more chili, for sour by adding more lime, for salty by adding more fish sauce and for sweet by adding more sugar.

Enjoy! Refrigerate leftovers in a sealed container for up to 3 days.

HOMEMADE SRIRACHA

The rooster brand sriracha that is ubiquitous has always been very acidic to me. Real Thai sriracha should balance heat, sweet and sour. This is my version and is fermented like the original Thai-style sriracha. Make sure the bowl or container that you are fermenting in is sterile or you could ruin the fermentation. I like to rinse the bowl with boiling water and allow it to air dry before fermenting.

MAKES: 3 CUPS (720 ML)

¾ lb (340 g) red jalapeno chilies, stemmed and roughly chopped

¼ lb (115 g) red serrano chilies, stemmed and roughly chopped

½ lb (226 g) green jalapeño chilies, stemmed and roughly chopped

4 cloves garlic

2 tbsp (30 g) white sugar

2 tbsp (28 g) palm sugar or brown sugar

1–2 tsp (5–10 g) kosher salt

½ cup (120 ml) distilled white vinegar

1 tsp xanthan gum (optional, to help stabilize the sauce for long holding)

Place the peppers, garlic, sugars and salt in a food processor and pulse until roughly chopped. Transfer the mixture to a clean container, cover and let sit at room temperature. A mason jar with a loosely fitting lid or a clean bowl with plastic wrap will work.

Fermentation should begin in about 2 days. When bubbles begin to form, stir your "mash" once or twice a day to combine and help it settle. Continue until the mixture stops bubbling, about 6 to 8 days.

Transfer the mash to a blender, add the vinegar, and puree until very smooth. Strain the sauce through a fine sieve. Add the xanthan gum and puree again until smooth and thick. Store your sauce in squeeze bottles in the fridge for up to 3 months.

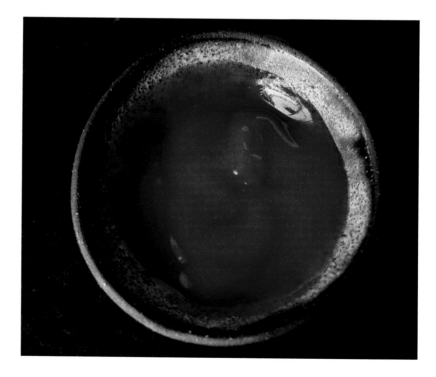

AJAD SAUCE

aka Cucumber Relish for Satay (Nam Jim Ajad)

This is the classic relish to pair with satay, featuring crisp cucumbers and red onion in a light sauce. I also love serving this on hot days with grilled meat. You can also slice the cucumbers large and serve it like a cucumber salad.

MAKES: ¾ CUP (180 ML)

½ cup (120 ml) white vinegar

¼ cup (60 ml) water

¼ cup (50 g) sugar

2 tsp (10 g) kosher salt

3 pickling cucumbers, peeled, quartered and thinly sliced

2 shallots, thinly sliced

1 Thai chili, thinly sliced

In a small saucepan over medium heat, combine the white vinegar, water, sugar, and salt. Bring the sauce to a simmer and stir until the sugar and salt are dissolved, about 2 minutes. Taste and adjust any of the seasonings if you'd like, then remove from the heat.

Pour the liquid into a medium bowl and allow it to cool slightly. Place the cucumbers, shallots, and chili into the sauce. Cover and refrigerate until ready to use, up to 2 weeks.

VINEGAR WITH CHILIES (Prik Nam Som)

This is one of the most popular table condiments in Thailand, only second to Fish Sauce with Chilies (page 205). A few drops of the vinegar with chilies are perfect for a little pop of acid and heat.

MAKES: 1 CUP (240 ML)

1 cup (240 ml) white vinegar

1 tsp sugar

½ tsp kosher salt

3 fresh serrano chilies, sliced ⅛ inch (3 mm) thick

1–2 cloves garlic, minced

In a small bowl, whisk together the vinegar, sugar and salt until the salt and sugar have completely dissolved.

Stir the chilies and garlic into the vinegar and let it infuse for at least 10 minutes before serving. Keep it refrigerated until ready to use, up to 2 weeks.

HOMEMADE SWEET CHILI SAUCE
(Nam Jim Gai)

Thai sweet chili sauce is universally loved and available in so many restaurants and even fast-food establishments. It's not always easy to find in markets, though, and I wanted to create a recipe that is easy to make at home. If you need to use sambal instead of chili-garlic sauce, use half the amount in the recipe as it's very spicy.

MAKES: ½ CUP (120 ML)

¼ tsp cayenne pepper

1 tsp cornstarch mixed with 2 tbsp (30 ml) water to make a slurry

1 clove garlic, minced

1½ tsp (8 g) kosher salt

2 tsp (10 ml) Chinese chili-garlic sauce

½ cup (100 g) sugar

¼ cup (60 ml) white vinegar

Stir together all the ingredients in a small saucepan until combined. Heat over medium heat until simmering and slightly thickened.

Remove the pan from the heat and allow the mixture to cool before serving. This sauce will keep in an airtight container at room temperature for up to 2 weeks.

ACKNOWLEDGMENTS

Jet's thank-yous:

Ali, Amaya and Ren Tila for always supporting every crazy idea I have. I love you all so very much.

Guy Fieri for taking the time to write the foreword and for decades of guidance and advice.

My mentors Alton Brown and Bobby Flay for your wisdom and guidance.

The team that made this book happen: Page Street Publishing team Sarah Demchuck, Ken Goodman and Will Kiester.

Team Tila: Taji Marie, Adam Contreras, Balo Orozco, Aubrey Devin, Meagan Van Deren and Mary Tila.

Jazz Singsanong, Tui Sungkamee and Alvin Petcha for culinary inspiration.

This book would not be the great work it is without you all. Thank you!

Tad's thank-yous:

Jet and Ali. I am truly grateful to my bosses who became my friends, my friends who became family. They are my champions, cheering squad, support system and patrons.

My immediate family. David and Myrtle, favorite sister Joni and her family, Jimmy, Nicole and Austin.

My extended family. Oshi Kiyabu, Rickey and Haruko and the Kiyabu family, the Higa family and all the aunties, uncles, cousins and Calabash relatives.

There are so many I wish to thank. Not just the individuals, but the teams and families supporting these fine people. My apologies to anyone I missed.

Neal Fraser and Amy Knoll Fraser at Redbird/Vibiana/Grace/BLD. Cecilia DeCastro & the Academy of Culinary Education, Amy of Amy's Culinary Adventures. Rene, Luis, Romiro and the team at Chinois on Main. Mega, Roy, Diana, Garbs, Adolfo, Francisco, Big Mike, Vidal, Mariah. Zoe & Josh at Huckleberry/RC. Mario Chavez. Jessica & team at SQIRL, Steve & Dina of Rossoblu. Jack McLaughlin of Jack's Catering. Mark Tydell. June and Manuel Cross. Aaron Diaz, Helen Cavallo at Food & Bounty. Balo Orozco at Sunset Cultures. Todd Radcliffe, Patch Troffer. Charlie Baggs at CBCI. Aarti Sequeira. Dan & Roxana at Friends & Family. Chris Kidder, Michael Drabkin. Peter & Lauren of Wax Paper Co/Lingua Franca, Tiffany & Tracy at BSB, Elayne at Catering Concierge. Andy-sensei at Sushi Chef Institute.

Love and respect to the farmers, ranchers, growers, makers, butchers and masters of their crafts.

My friends. Tim Smith, Colleen & the Campbell family, Missy and the Reitner family, Tracy and the Feldstein family, Chad & the Shibuya family, Janelle and the Valera family, Mark and the Kim family. Eugene and the Tan family, Mary at HailM Cocktails. Iqbal, Jeffro, Bethro, Scott and the Donnell family, Brody & the Schiess family. Melissa Monroe. Michael, Caroline and Steven, the Lau Family, the Robles family, Steve and the Kenton family, Richard Velasco, Ara and the Mgrdichian family, Kevo and the Sassouni family. Paola. Frank Casares at Surfas, Doug and the Yee family, George Uch. Aziz & the Nabil family, Ayoubb, Dris, Imad. Tara Stevens. Amber Faith. Jon Broida at JKI, Barbecue_Mike Lee.

Rest in Paradise Denise Ruff and Javier Esquivel.

ABOUT THE AUTHORS

Jet Tila is a James Beard, Emmy & People's Choice–nominated chef. Jet is internationally recognized for his culinary expertise in modern Asian cuisine. He grew up in Los Angeles's Thai Town, home to the largest Thai population outside of Thailand (roughly 80,000 of California's estimated 120,000 Thai Americans live in Los Angeles). Tila learned the ancient traditions of Asian cuisine from his Cantonese grandmother while lending a hand at his family's famed Bangkok Market—the first Thai market to open in the United States in the 1970s—and Royal Thai restaurant. Tila's culinary curiosity has allowed him to experience multiple endeavors, from opening Wazuzu at the Wynn Las Vegas in a record 98 days to partnering with Compass Group, the world's largest food-service company.

Celebrated as a culinary luminary, Tila was appointed as the inaugural Culinary Ambassador of Thai Cuisine by the Royal Thai Consulate-General, Los Angeles, and is the first-ever chef to officially represent his country's culture and cuisine in the United States.

Tila was featured in the *New York Times* dining section cover story as a "culinary storyteller." He is also known for having set multiple Guinness culinary world records. He's made recurring celebrity chef appearances on *Cutthroat Kitchen*, *Guy's Grocery Games*, *Iron Chef America*, *Chopped*, *The Best Thing I Ever Ate* (Giada De Laurentiis chose his Drunken Noodles [page 51] as the best thing she ever ate with chopsticks), *Anthony Bourdain's No Reservations* and CNN's *Parts Unknown*. Additionally, in May 2013, Tila was honored with the prestigious Dream of Los Angeles Award by the City of Los Angeles for igniting a renewed interest in Pan-Asian cuisine through dedication to his Thai and Chinese roots and passion for the culinary arts inside and outside the kitchen.

Tad Weyland Fukumoto is a nationally recognized chef, culinary producer and consultant. He was born and raised in Hawaii to a long line of great cooks, surrounded by rich culinary cultures including Chinese, Japanese and Okinawan cuisines. After attending university in Northern California, he moved to Los Angeles to pursue his passion for music while always having a hand in the LA food scene. After a few years spending his days in music and nights cooking in some of LA's best restaurants, the kitchen lured Tad to switch careers. Tad attended the Academy of Culinary Education and his culinary CV includes acclaimed restaurants such as Wazuzu @ Encore/Wynn Las Vegas, Grace, BLD, Chinois on Main and Sqirl. Tad and Jet have been best friends and collaborators for more than twenty years.

INDEX

A

Ajad Sauce, 207

Anaheim chili peppers, in Northern Thai Eggplant and Chili Dip, 184

Angel Wings, 140–142

apples
Crispy Catfish Raft Salad With Green Mango, 127
Deep-Fried Trout With Green Mango Slaw, 129
Thai Yum Rice Salad, 162

apps & small plates
Chicken Satay, 149
Fried Thai Fish Cakes, 152
Fried Wontons, 139
Grilled Pork Sticks, 138
Isaan Chicken Laarb, 146
Roti Bread, 143–145
Savory Pork Jerky, 153
Stuffed Chicken Wings, Aka Angel Wings, 140–142
Thai Crispy Spring Rolls, 137
Thai Savory Bites, 151
Thai-Style Steamed Dumplings, 150

B

bamboo shoots
Panang Curry Chicken, 22
Vegan Yellow Curry, 173

basil
about, 14
Clams in Roasted Chili Sauce, 124
Drunken Noodles, 51
Fried Thai Fish Cakes, 152
Green Curry Paste, 29
Hai Yai Fried Chicken, 96
Panang Curry Chicken, 22
Roast Duck Red Curry, 25
Spicy Basil Stir-Fry, 111

Spicy Basil Tofu Stir-Fry, 169
Steamed Mussels With Thai Herbs in Spicy Broth, 133
Street-Style Basil Pork, 65
Vegan Drunken Noodles, 176
Vegan Yellow Curry, 173

bean sprouts
Beef Boat Noodle Soup, 37
My Classic Pad Thai, 46
Vegan Pad Thai, 175
Bean Sprouts Stir-Fried With Fried Tofu, 163

beef
Beef Boat Noodle Soup, 37
Garlic Pepper Beef Stir-Fry, 101
Heavenly Beef Jerky, 112
Isaan-Style Waterfall Beef, 107
Lard Nar Noodles, 47
Massaman Beef Curry, 26
New Beef Satay, 109
Northern Braised Beef Curry Noodles, 102
Spicy Basil Stir-Fry, 111
Thai Beef Salad, 157
Thai Braised Beef Short Ribs, 110
Beef Boat Noodle Soup, 37

bell peppers
Fried Tilapia With Three-Flavor Sauce, 130
New Prik King Chicken, 90
Panang Curry Chicken, 22
Roast Duck Red Curry, 25
Spicy Basil Stir-Fry, 111
Spicy Basil Tofu Stir-Fry, 169
Thai Cashew Chicken, 86
Vegan Yellow Curry, 173

broccoli
Chicken Pad See Ew, 48
Lard Nar Noodles, 47
Vegan Pad See Ew, 170
broccoli, Chinese
Lard Nar Noodles, 47
Stir-Fried Chinese Broccoli, 181
Stir-Fried Chinese Broccoli With Crispy Pork Belly, 74

Thai Street-Style Chicken Fried Rice, 61
Thai Vegan Fried Rice, 179

C

cabbage
Coconut Chicken Soup, 38
Glass Noodle Stir-Fry, 54
Northern Thai Pork and Tomato Chili Dip, 104
Vegan Coconut Galanga Soup, 172
Vegan Tofu Larb, 180

Cafe Yen, 200

carrots
Northern Thai Pork and Tomato Chili Dip, 104
Stuffed Chicken Wings, Aka Angel Wings, 140
Thai Crispy Spring Rolls, 137
Thai-Style Steamed Dumplings, 150
Vegan Tofu Larb, 180

cashews
Coconut Mango Salad With Shrimp, 156
Crispy Catfish Raft Salad With Green Mango, 127
Deep-Fried Trout With Green Mango Slaw, 129
Thai Cashew Chicken, 86
Thai Yum Rice Salad, 162
Catfish Raft Salad With Green Mango, Crispy, 127

celery
Crispy Catfish Raft Salad With Green Mango, 127
Glass Noodle Stir-Fry, 54
Thai Braised Beef Short Ribs, 110

Cha Nom Yen, 199

chicken
Chicken Pad See Ew, 48
Chicken Satay, 149
Coconut Chicken Soup, 38
Crispy Sticky Tamarind Noodles, 53
Glass Noodle Stir-Fry, 54
Hai Yai Fried Chicken, 95–96
Hainan Chicken Rice, 93–94
Isaan Chicken Laarb, 146

My Classic Pad Thai, 45
New Prik King Chicken, 90
New Thai BBQ Chicken, 85
Northern Curry Chicken With Noodles, 97
Panang Curry Chicken, 22
Pan-Fried Rice Noodles With Chicken and Squid, 50
Pineapple Fried Rice, 66
Thai Cashew Chicken, 86
Thai Chicken Stock, 41
Thai Street-Style Chicken Fried Rice, 61
Chicken Pad See Ew, 48
Chicken Satay, 149
Chicken Wings, Stuffed, 140–142
chili paste in soybean oil (*Nam Prik Pow*), 14
chili peppers, 15, 28
Chili Sauce, 93
chilies de arbol
Coconut Chicken Soup, 38
Crispy Rice Salad, 70
Massaman Curry Paste, 33
Panang Curry Paste, 32
Red Curry Paste, 29
Shrimp Tom Yum Soup, 34
Stir-Fried Chinese Broccoli, 181
Stir-Fried Chinese Broccoli With Crispy Pork Belly, 74
chilies, Fresno
Clams in Roasted Chili Sauce, 124
Fried Tilapia With Three-Flavor Sauce, 130
Red Curry Paste, 29
chilies, guajillo
Massaman Curry Paste, 33
Panang Curry Paste, 32
Yellow Curry Paste, 32
chilies, jalapeño
Clams in Roasted Chili Sauce, 124
Homemade Sriracha, 206
Red Curry Paste, 29
chilies, Japones
Massaman Curry Paste, 33
Panang Curry Paste, 32
Red Curry Paste, 29
chilies, serrano (prik-cheefa)
about, 15

Drunken Noodles, 51

Green Curry Paste, 29

Homemade Sriracha, 206

Spicy Basil Stir-Fry, 111

Spicy Basil Tofu Stir-Fry, 169

Vegan Drunken Noodles, 176

Vinegar With Chilies, 207

chilies, Thai

Clams in Roasted Chili Sauce, 124

Coconut Chicken Soup, 38

Coconut Mango Salad With Shrimp, 156

Crispy Morning Glory Salad, 160

Deep-Fried Trout With Green Mango Slaw, 129

Duck Salad With Lychee, 89

Isaan Chicken Laarb, 146

Isaan-Style Waterfall Beef, 107

Northern Thai Eggplant and Chili Dip, 184

Northern Thai Pork and Tomato Chili Dip, 104

Northern Thai Sausage, 117

Papaya Salad, 159

Shrimp Tom Yum Soup, 34

Spicy Basil Stir-Fry, 111

Spicy Basil Tofu Stir-Fry, 169

Steamed Mussels With Thai Herbs in Spicy Broth, 133

Stir-Fried Chinese Broccoli, 181

Street-Style Basil Pork, 65

Thai Cashew Chicken, 86

Thai Chicken Stock, 41

Thai Savory Bites, 151

Thai Yum Rice Salad, 162

Vegan Coconut Galanga Soup, 172

Yum Dressing, 127

chilies, Thai bird (prik-keenu)

about, 15

Fish Sauce With Chilies, 205

Morning Glory on Fire, 165

Stir-Fried Chinese Broccoli, 181

Stir-Fried Chinese Broccoli With Crispy Pork Belly, 74

Chinese chicken powder

Coconut Chicken Soup, 38

Shrimp Tom Yum Soup, 34

Thai Rice Porridge With Pork Meatballs and Coddled Egg, 40

cilantro

Beef Boat Noodle Soup, 37

Crispy Catfish Raft Salad With Green Mango, 127

Crispy Morning Glory Salad, 160

Crispy Rice Salad, 70

Deep-Fried Trout With Green Mango Slaw, 129

Glass Noodle Stir-Fry, 54

Green Curry Paste, 29

Grilled Pork Sticks, 138

Hainan Chicken Rice, 94

Isaan-Style Waterfall Beef, 107

Northern Braised Beef Curry Noodles, 102

Northern Thai Pork and Tomato Chili Dip, 104

Northern Thai Sausage, 117

Pineapple Fried Rice, 66

Steamed Mussels With Thai Herbs in Spicy Broth, 133

Thai Beef Salad, 157

Thai Yum Rice Salad, 162

Clams in Roasted Chili Sauce, 124

coconut

Coconut Mango Salad With Shrimp, 156

Crispy Rice Salad, 69

Thai Savory Bites, 151

Coconut Chicken Soup, 38

Coconut Mango Salad With Shrimp, 156

coconut milk/cream

about, 12

Chicken Satay, 149

Coconut Chicken Soup, 38

Coconut Sticky Rice With Mango, 196

Coconut Syrup, 76

Crispy Morning Glory Salad, 160

Massaman Beef Curry, 26–27

New Beef Satay, 109

New Thai BBQ Chicken, 85

Northern Braised Beef Curry Noodles, 102

Northern Curry Chicken With Noodles, 97

Panang Curry Chicken, 22

Pandan Sweet Sticky Rice, 76–77

Roast Duck Red Curry, 25

Steamed Coconut Custard in Kabocha Squash, 191

Sweet Coconut Milk Pancakes, 192

Thai Crepes With Pandan Cream, 195

Thai Peanut Sauce, 204

Tofu Satay, 182

Vegan Coconut Galanga Soup, 172

Vegan Peanut Sauce, 185

Vegan Yellow Curry, 173

Coconut Sticky Rice With Mango, 196

Coconut Syrup, 76

condiments. See sauces, dips & condiments

Crispy Catfish Raft Salad With Green Mango, 127–128

Crispy Morning Glory Salad, 160

Crispy Pork Belly, 114

Crispy Rice Salad, 69–70

Crispy Sticky Tamarind Noodles, 53

Cucumber Relish, 207

cucumbers

Ajad Sauce, 207

Duck Salad With Lychee, 89

Hainan Chicken Rice, 94

Northern Thai Eggplant and Chili Dip, 184

Northern Thai Pork and Tomato Chili Dip, 104

Thai Beef Salad, 157

cumin

Green Curry Paste, 29

Hai Yai Fried Chicken, 95

Heavenly Beef Jerky, 112

Massaman Curry Paste, 33

Panang Curry Paste, 32

Yellow Curry Paste, 32

curries & soups

Beef Boat Noodle Soup, 37

Coconut Chicken Soup, 38

Massaman Beef Curry, 26–27

My Favorite Northern Curry, 21

Panang Curry Chicken, 22

Roast Duck Red Curry, 25

Shrimp Tom Yum Soup, 34

Thai Chicken Stock, 41

Thai Rice Porridge With Pork Meatballs and Coddled Egg, 40

Vegan Yellow Curry, 173

curry pastes

about, 13, 28

Green Curry Paste, 29

Massaman Curry Paste, 33

Panang Curry Paste, 32

Red Curry Paste, 29

Yellow Curry Paste, 32

D

Deep-Fried Trout With Green Mango Slaw, 129

dips. See sauces, dips & condiments

Drunken Noodles, 51

Duck Red Curry, Roast, 21

Duck Salad With Lychee, 89

E

egg noodles

about, 15

Northern Braised Beef Curry Noodles, 102

Northern Curry Chicken With Noodles, 97

Eggplant and Chili Dip, Northern Thai, 184

eggs

Chicken Pad See Ew, 48

Crispy Rice Salad, 69

Deep-Fried Trout With Green Mango Slaw, 129

Drunken Noodles, 51

Egg Thread omelet, 73

Fried Thai Fish Cakes, 152

Glass Noodle Stir-Fry, 54

Minced Pork Thai Omelet, 113

My Classic Pad Thai, 45

Pan-Fried Rice Noodles With Chicken and Squid, 50

Steamed Coconut Custard in Kabocha Squash, 191

Stuffed Chicken Wings, Aka Angel Wings, 140

Thai Crepes With Pandan Cream, 195

Thai Omelet, 73

Thai Rice Porridge With Pork Meatballs and Coddled Egg, 40

Thai Shrimp Cakes, 123

Thai Street-Style Chicken Fried Rice, 61

F

Faktong Sangkaya, 191

Fermented Soy Dipping Sauce, 93

fish fillets

Crispy Catfish Raft Salad With Green Mango, 127

Deep-Fried Trout With Green Mango Slaw, 129

Fried Thai Fish Cakes, 152

Fried Tilapia With Three-Flavor Sauce, 130

fish sauce, 13

Fish Sauce With Chilies, 205

Fresh Rice Noodles, 56–57

Fried Thai Fish Cakes, 152

Fried Tilapia With Three-Flavor Sauce, 130

Fried Wontons, 139

G

Gaeng Hung Lay Moo, 25

Gaeng Massamun Neau, 26

Gaeng Panang Gai, 22

Gaeng Phed Ped Yang, 21

Gai Pad Med Mamuang Himaphan, 86

Gai Taud Hat Yai, 95–96

Gai Yang, 85

galanga (Kha)

about, 15

Coconut Chicken Soup, 38

Green Curry Paste, 29

Massaman Beef Curry, 26

Massaman Curry Paste, 33

Northern Thai Sausage, 117

Panang Curry Paste, 32

Red Curry Paste, 29

Shrimp Tom Yum Soup, 34

Steamed Mussels With Thai Herbs in Spicy Broth, 133

Thai Chicken Stock, 41

Thai Savory Bites, 151

Vegan Coconut Galanga Soup, 172

Yellow Curry Paste, 32

Gang Leung Jay, 173

Garlic Pepper Beef Stir-Fry, 101

Ginger Garlic Sauce, 94

glass noodles (bean thread)

about, 16

Glass Noodle Stir-Fry, 54

Stuffed Chicken Wings, Aka Angel Wings, 140

Thai Crispy Spring Rolls, 137

Grandma's Everything Dipping Sauce, 205

grapeseed oil, 12

Green Curry Paste, 29

green/long beans

Fried Thai Fish Cakes, 152

New Prik King Chicken, 90

Northern Thai Eggplant and Chili Dip, 184

Papaya Salad, 159

Street-Style Basil Pork, 65

Vegan Tofu Larb, 180

Grilled Pork Sticks, 138

H

Hai Yai Fried Chicken, 95–96

Hainan Chicken Rice, 93–94

Heavenly Beef Jerky, 112

Homemade Sriracha, 206

Homemade Sweet Chili Sauce, 208

Hoy Lai Pad Prik Pao, 124

Hoy Malaengphoo Nung, 133

I

Isaan Chicken Laarb, 146

Isaan-Style Waterfall Beef, 107

J

jasmine rice

about, 16

brown, 79

Crispy Rice Salad, 69

Hainan Chicken Rice, 94

Pineapple Fried Rice, 66

preparing, 79

Shrimp Paste Fried Rice, 62

Thai Rice Porridge With Pork Meatballs and Coddled Egg, 40

Thai Street-Style Chicken Fried Rice, 61

Thai Vegan Fried Rice, 179

Thai Yum Rice Salad, 162

white, 79

Jok Moo, 40

K

Kabocha Squash, Steamed Coconut Custard in, 191

kaffir lime leaves, 15

Kanom Jeeb, 150

Kanom Krok, 192

Kauy Teow Sen Yai, 56–57

Keow Taud, 139

Khai Jiao, 73

Khai Jiao Moo Sab, 113

Khana Moo Krob, 74

Khanom Tokyo, 195

Khao Hom Mali, 79

Khao Khluk Kapi, 62

Khao Man Gai, 93–94

Khao Neow, 80

Khao Neow Mamuang, 196

Khao Neow Moon Bai Toey, 76–77

Khao Pad Gai, 61

Khao Pad Jay, 179

Khao Pad Sapparod, 66

Khao Soi Gai, 97

Khao Soi Neau Toon, 102

Khao Yum, 162

Krapow Moo Sap, 65

Krapow Taohu, 169

Kuay Teow Gai Kua, 50

Kuay Teow Lard Nar, 47

Kuaytiaw Reua, 37

L

Laap Gai Isaan, 146

Lard Nar Noodles, 47

lemongrass (Takhi), 15

lettuce

Duck Salad With Lychee, 89

Pan-Fried Rice Noodles With Chicken and Squid, 50

Thai Beef Salad, 157

Vegan Tofu Larb, 180

long beans. See green/long beans

Lychee, Duck Salad With, 89

M

mangoes

Coconut Mango Salad With Shrimp, 156

Coconut Sticky Rice With Mango, 196

Crispy Catfish Raft Salad With Green Mango, 127

Deep-Fried Trout With Green Mango Slaw, 129

Thai Yum Rice Salad, 162

Massaman Beef Curry, 26–27

massaman curry paste

Massaman Beef Curry, 27

Northern Braised Beef Curry Noodles, 102

Northern Curry Chicken With Noodles, 97

recipe for, 33

Mee Krob, 53

Miang Kham, 151

Minced Pork Thai Omelet, 113

mint leaves

Duck Salad With Lychee, 89

Isaan-Style Waterfall Beef, 107

Thai Beef Salad, 157

Thai Yum Rice Salad, 162

Vegan Tofu Larb, 180

Moo Dang, 105

Moo Dat Diow, 153

Moo Krob, 114

Moo Ping, 138

Moo Wan, 108

morning glory
- Beef Boat Noodle Soup, 37
- Crispy Morning Glory Salad, 160
- Morning Glory on Fire, 165

msg (monosodium glutamate), 13–14

mushrooms
- Coconut Chicken Soup, 38
- Shrimp Tom Yum Soup, 34
- Stuffed Chicken Wings, Aka Angel Wings, 140
- Thai Crispy Spring Rolls, 137
- Thai-Style Steamed Dumplings, 150
- Vegan Coconut Galanga Soup, 172

Mussels With Thai Herbs in Spicy Broth, Steamed, 133

mustard greens, Chinese pickled
- Northern Braised Beef Curry Noodles, 102
- Northern Curry Chicken With Noodles, 97

My Classic Pad Thai, 45–46

My Favorite Northern Curry, 21

N

Nam Jim Ajad, 207
Nam Jim Gai, 208
Nam Jim Satay, 204
Nam Jim Satay Jay, 185
Nam Khao Tod, 69–70
Nam Prik Noom, 184
Nam Prik Ong, 104
Nam Prik Pow, 14
Nam Tok Neau, 107
Neau Satay, 109
Neau Sawan, 112
Neau Toon, 110
New Beef Satay, 109
New Prik King Chicken, 90
New Thai BBQ Chicken, 85

noodle dishes
- Chicken Pad See Ew, 48
- Crispy Sticky Tamarind Noodles, 53
- Drunken Noodles, 51
- Fresh Rice Noodles, 56–57
- Glass Noodle Stir-Fry, 54
- Lard Nar Noodles, 47
- My Classic Pad Thai, 45–46
- Northern Braised Beef Curry Noodles, 102
- Northern Curry Chicken With Noodles, 97
- Pan-Fried Rice Noodles With Chicken and Squid, 50
- Vegan Drunken Noodles, 176
- Vegan Pad See Ew, 170

noodles, 15–16
Northern Braised Beef Curry Noodles, 102
Northern Curry Chicken With Noodles, 97
Northern Thai Eggplant and Chili Dip, 184
Northern Thai Pork and Tomato Chili Dip, 104
Northern Thai Sausage, 117–118
Nua Tod Kratiem Prik Thai, 101

O

oils, 12
oyster sauce, 14

P

Pad Kee Mow, 51
Pad Kee Mow Jay, 176
Pad Khana, 181
Pad Krapow Neau Sap, 111
Pad See Ew Gai, 48
Pad See Ew Jay, 170
Pad Thai
- My Classic Pad Thai, 45–46
- noodles for, 16
- Vegan Pad Thai, 175
Pad Thai Jay, 175
Pad Thai Sauce, 45
Pad Woon Sen, 54
Pak Boong Fai Dang, 165
palm sugar, 191
Panang Curry Chicken, 22
Panang Curry Paste, 32
Pandan Cream, 195

pandan leaves
- Coconut Syrup, 76
- Pandan Sweet Sticky Rice, 76
- Steamed Coconut Custard in Kabocha Squash, 191
- Thai Crepes With Pandan Cream, 195
Pandan Sweet Sticky Rice, 76–77
Pan-Fried Rice Noodles With Chicken and Squid, 50

panko breadcrumbs
- Deep-Fried Trout With Green Mango Slaw, 129
- Stuffed Chicken Wings, Aka Angel Wings, 140
- Thai Shrimp Cakes, 123
Papaya Salad, 159

peanut butter
- Thai Peanut Sauce, 204
- Vegan Peanut Sauce, 185

peanuts
- Crispy Catfish Raft Salad With Green Mango, 127
- Crispy Morning Glory Salad, 160
- Crispy Rice Salad, 70
- Massaman Beef Curry, 27
- My Classic Pad Thai, 46
- My Favorite Northern Curry, 21
- Papaya Salad, 159
- Thai Savory Bites, 151
- Vegan Pad Thai, 175
Peek Gai Yat Sai, 140–142

pineapples
- Pineapple Fried Rice, 66
- Roast Duck Red Curry, 25
Pla Taud Mamuang Yum, 129
Pla Tub Tim Thod Sam Rod, 130

plant-based Thai
- Northern Thai Eggplant and Chili Dip, 184
- Spicy Basil Tofu Stir-Fry, 169
- Stir-Fried Chinese Broccoli, 181
- Thai Vegan Fried Rice, 179
- Tofu Satay, 182
- Vegan Coconut Galanga Soup, 172
- Vegan Drunken Noodles, 176
- Vegan Pad See Ew, 170
- Vegan Pad Thai, 175
- Vegan Peanut Sauce, 185
- Vegan Tofu Larb, 180
- Vegan Yellow Curry, 173
Popia Taud, 137

pork
- Grilled Pork Sticks, 138
- My Favorite Northern Curry, 21
- Northern Thai Sausage, 117
- Red Roasted Pork, 105
- Savory Pork Jerky, 153

pork belly
- Crispy Pork Belly, 114
- My Favorite Northern Curry, 21
- Stir-Fried Chinese Broccoli With Crispy Pork Belly, 74
- Thai Sweet Pork, 108
pork cracklings, in Northern Thai Pork and Tomato Chili Dip, 104

pork, ground
- Crispy Rice Salad, 69–70
- Fried Wontons, 139
- Minced Pork Thai Omelet, 113
- Northern Thai Pork and Tomato Chili Dip, 104
- Pork Meatballs, 40
- Street-Style Basil Pork, 65
- Stuffed Chicken Wings, Aka Angel Wings, 140
- Thai Crispy Spring Rolls, 137
- Thai Shrimp Cakes, 123
- Thai-Style Steamed Dumplings, 150
Pork Meatballs, 40
potatoes, in Massaman Beef Curry, 27
Prik Gaeng Dang, 29
Prik Gaeng Keow, 29
Prik Gaeng Leung, 32
Prik Gaeng Massamun, 33
Prik Gaeng Panang, 32
Prik King Chicken, 90
Prik King Gai, 90
Prik Nam Pla, 205
Prik Nam Som, 207

R

radish, in My Classic Pad
Thai, 45
red curry paste
Chicken Satay, 149
Crispy Rice Salad, 69
Fried Thai Fish Cakes, 152
My Favorite Northern
Curry, 21
New Thai BBQ Chicken,
85
Northern Thai Pork and
Tomato Chili Dip, 104
recipe for, 29
Roast Duck Red Curry, 25
Thai Peanut Sauce, 204
Tofu Satay, 182
Vegan Peanut Sauce, 185
Red Roasted Pork, 105
rice. See also jasmine rice
about, 16
brown jasmine, 79
jasmine, 16, 79
Thai sticky, 16, 80
white jasmine, 79
Rice Balls, 69
rice cookers, 79
rice dishes
Brown Jasmine Rice, 79
Coconut Sticky Rice With
Mango, 196
Crispy Rice Salad, 69–70
Hainan Chicken Rice,
93–94
Pandan Sweet Sticky Rice,
76–77
Pineapple Fried Rice, 66
Shrimp Paste Fried Rice,
62
Stir-Fried Chinese Broc-
coli With Crispy Pork
Belly, 74
Street-Style Basil Pork, 65
Thai Omelet, 73
Thai Sticky Rice, 80
Thai Street-Style Chicken
Fried Rice, 61
Thai Vegan Fried Rice, 179
Thai Yum Rice Salad, 162
White Jasmine Rice, 79
rice flour
Fresh Rice Noodles, 56

Sweet Coconut Milk Pan-
cakes, 192
rice noodles
Chicken Pad See Ew, 48
Drunken Noodles, 51
Fresh Rice Noodles, 56–57
Lard Nar Noodles, 47
Pan-Fried Rice Noodles
With Chicken and Squid,
50
Vegan Drunken Noodles,
176
Vegan Pad See Ew, 170
Vegan Pad Thai, 175
Rice Porridge, 40
rice powder, roasted
about, 15
Isaan Chicken Laarb, 146
Isaan-Style Waterfall Beef,
107
recipe for, 180
Thai Shrimp Cakes, 123
Vegan Tofu Larb, 180
rice stick noodles
about, 16
Beef Boat Noodle Soup,
37
Crispy Sticky Tamarind
Noodles, 53
My Classic Pad Thai, 45
Roast Duck Red Curry, 25
roasted chili paste, 14. See
also chili paste in soybean
oil (Nam Prik Pow)
Roti Bread
Panang Curry Chicken, 22
recipe for, 143–145

S

Sai Ua, 117–118
salads & umami veggies
Bean Sprouts Stir-Fried
With Fried Tofu, 163
Coconut Mango Salad
With Shrimp, 156
Crispy Catfish Raft Salad
With Green Mango,
127–128
Crispy Morning Glory
Salad, 160
Crispy Rice Salad, 69
Duck Salad With Lychee,
89
Morning Glory on Fire, 165
Papaya Salad, 159

Thai Beef Salad, 157
Thai Yum Rice Salad, 162
Satay Gai, 149
sauces, dips & condiments
Ajad Sauce, 207
Chili Sauce, 93
Fermented Soy Dipping
Sauce, 93
Fish Sauce With Chilies,
205
Ginger Garlic Sauce, 94
Grandma's Everything
Dipping Sauce, 205
Homemade Sriracha, 206
Homemade Sweet Chili
Sauce, 208
Northern Thai Eggplant
and Chili Dip, 184
Thai Peanut Sauce, 204
Vegan Peanut Sauce, 185
Vinegar With Chilies, 207
Yum Dressing, 127
sausages
Crispy Rice Salad, 70
Northern Thai Sausage,
117–118
Pineapple Fried Rice, 66
Savory Pork Jerky, 153
scallions
Bean Sprouts Stir-Fried
With Fried Tofu, 163
Coconut Mango Salad
With Shrimp, 156
Crispy Rice Salad, 70
Fried Tilapia With
Three-Flavor Sauce, 130
Ginger Garlic Sauce, 94
Glass Noodle Stir-Fry, 54
Minced Pork Thai Omelet,
113
My Classic Pad Thai, 46
Northern Braised Beef
Curry Noodles, 102
Northern Thai Pork and
Tomato Chili Dip, 104
Pan-Fried Rice Noodles
With Chicken and Squid,
50
Pineapple Fried Rice, 66
Thai Beef Salad, 157
Thai Crispy Spring Rolls,
137
Thai Yum Rice Salad, 162
Vegan Pad Thai, 175
Vegan Tofu Larb, 180
seafood dishes
Clams in Roasted Chili

Sauce, 124
Coconut Mango Salad
With Shrimp, 156
Crispy Catfish Raft Salad
With Green Mango,
127–128
Crispy Morning Glory
Salad, 160
Crispy Sticky Tamarind
Noodles, 53
Deep-Fried Trout With
Green Mango Slaw, 129
Drunken Noodles, 51
Fried Thai Fish Cakes, 152
Fried Tilapia With
Three-Flavor Sauce, 130
My Classic Pad Thai,
45–46
Shrimp Tom Yum Soup, 34
Steamed Mussels With
Thai Herbs in Spicy
Broth, 133
Thai Shrimp Cakes, 123
sesame seeds, in Heavenly
Beef Jerky, 112
shallots
Ajad Sauce, 207
Coconut Mango Salad
With Shrimp, 156
Crispy Rice Salad, 70
Deep-Fried Trout With
Green Mango Slaw, 129
Hai Yai Fried Chicken, 96
Isaan Chicken Laarb, 146
Isaan-Style Waterfall Beef,
107
Massaman Curry Paste, 33
Northern Braised Beef
Curry Noodles, 102
Northern Curry Chicken
With Noodles, 97
Northern Thai Eggplant
and Chili Dip, 184
Northern Thai Sausage, 117
Panang Curry Paste, 32
Pineapple Fried Rice, 66
Red Curry Paste, 29
Stuffed Chicken Wings,
Aka Angel Wings, 140
Thai Braised Beef Short
Ribs, 110
Thai Chicken Stock, 41
Thai Crispy Spring Rolls,
137
Thai Savory Bites, 151
Thai Sweet Pork, 108
Thai Yum Rice Salad, 162
Vegan Tofu Larb, 180

Yellow Curry Paste, 32

shrimp

Coconut Mango Salad With Shrimp, 156

Crispy Morning Glory Salad, 160

Crispy Sticky Tamarind Noodles, 53

Drunken Noodles, 51

Fried Wontons, 139

My Classic Pad Thai, 45–46

Shrimp Tom Yum Soup, 34

Thai Shrimp Cakes, 123

Thai-Style Steamed Dumplings, 150

shrimp, dried

My Classic Pad Thai, 45

Thai Savory Bites, 151

Thai Yum Rice Salad, 162

shrimp paste

Green Curry Paste, 29

Massaman Beef Curry, 27

Massaman Curry Paste, 33

Panang Curry Paste, 32

Red Curry Paste, 29

Shrimp Paste Fried Rice, 62

Thai Savory Bites, 151

Yellow Curry Paste, 32

Shrimp Tom Yum Soup, 34

Som Tum Thai, 159

soups

Beef Boat Noodle Soup, 37

Coconut Chicken Soup, 38

Shrimp Tom Yum Soup, 34

Thai Chicken Stock, 41

Thai Rice Porridge With Pork Meatballs and Coddled Egg, 40

Vegan Coconut Galanga Soup, 172

soy sauce, 11–12

Spicy Basil Stir-Fry, 111

Spicy Basil Tofu Stir-Fry, 169

Squid, Pan-Fried Rice Noodles With Chicken and, 50

sriracha, 14

Steamed Coconut Custard in Kabocha Squash, 191

Steamed Mussels With Thai Herbs in Spicy Broth, 133

Stir-Fried Chinese Broccoli, 181

Stir-Fried Chinese Broccoli

With Crispy Pork Belly, 74

Street-Style Basil Pork, 65

Stuffed Chicken Wings, Aka Angel Wings, 140–142

Sweet Coconut Milk Pancakes, 192

sweets

Coconut Sticky Rice With Mango, 196

Steamed Coconut Custard in Kabocha Squash, 191

Sweet Coconut Milk Pancakes, 192

Thai Crepes With Pandan Cream, 195

Thai Iced Coffee, 200

Thai Iced Tea, 199

T

Taohu Lap, 180

Taohu Satay, 182

Thai Beef Salad, 157

Thai Braised Beef Short Ribs, 110

Thai Cashew Chicken, 86

Thai Chicken Stock, 41

Thai Crepes With Pandan Cream, 195

Thai Crispy Spring Rolls, 137

Thai Iced Coffee, 200

Thai Iced Tea, 199

Thai Omelet, 73

Thai Peanut Sauce, 204

Thai Rice Porridge With Pork Meatballs and Coddled Egg, 40

Thai Savory Bites, 151

Thai Shrimp Cakes, 123

Thai soybean sauce, 12

Thai Sticky Rice, 16, 80

Thai Street-Style Chicken Fried Rice, 61

Thai Sweet Pork, 108

Thai Vegan Fried Rice, 179

Thai Yum Rice Salad, 162

Thai-Style Steamed Dumplings, 150

Thua Ngok Pad Taohu, 163

Tilapia With Three-Flavor Sauce, Fried, 130

Tod Mun Goong, 123

Tod Mun Pla, 152

tofu

Bean Sprouts Stir-Fried With Fried Tofu, 163

Crispy Sticky Tamarind Noodles, 53

My Classic Pad Thai, 45

Spicy Basil Tofu Stir-Fry, 169

Thai Vegan Fried Rice, 179

Tofu Satay, 182

Vegan Coconut Galanga Soup, 172

Vegan Drunken Noodles, 176

Vegan Pad See Ew, 170

Vegan Pad Thai, 175

Vegan Tofu Larb, 180

Vegan Yellow Curry, 173

Tofu Satay, 182

Tom Kha Gai, 38

Tom Kha Jay, 172

Tom Yum Goong, 34

tomato paste

Crispy Sticky Tamarind Noodles, 53

Northern Thai Pork and Tomato Chili Dip, 104

tomatoes

Drunken Noodles, 51

Glass Noodle Stir-Fry, 54

Northern Thai Pork and Tomato Chili Dip, 104

Papaya Salad, 159

Roast Duck Red Curry, 25

Thai Street-Style Chicken Fried Rice, 61

Thai Vegan Fried Rice, 179

Vegan Drunken Noodles, 176

Trout With Green Mango Slaw, Deep-Fried, 129

turnip, sweet pickled, in Vegan Pad Thai, 175

V

Vegan Coconut Galanga Soup, 172

vegan dishes. See plant-based Thai

Vegan Drunken Noodles, 176

Vegan Pad See Ew, 170

Vegan Pad Thai, 175

Vegan Peanut Sauce, 185

Vegan Tofu Larb, 180

Vegan Yellow Curry, 173

vegetable base paste, in Vegan Coconut Galanga Soup, 172

vegetable dishes. See plant-based Thai; salads & umami veggies

Vinegar With Chilies, 207

W

woks, 17

wonton skins

Fried Wontons, 139

Thai-Style Steamed Dumplings, 150

Y

yellow bean sauce

about, 14

Lard Nar Noodles, 47

yellow curry paste

Northern Braised Beef Curry Noodles, 102

Northern Curry Chicken With Noodles, 97

recipe for, 32

Vegan Yellow Curry, 173

yellow soybean paste, in Morning Glory on Fire, 165

Yum Dressing, 127

Yum Mamuang, 156

Yum Neua, 157

Yum Pak Boong, 160

Yum Ped Yang Linchee, 89

Yum Pla Duk Foo, 127–128